Productions in Print
An In An Hour Book
www.inanhourbooks.com
An imprint of Smith and Kraus Publishers, Inc.
Published by Smith and Kraus, Inc.
177 Lyme Road, Hanover, NH 03755
www.SmithandKraus.com

LOMBARDI
by
Eric Simonson

Manufactured in the United States of America, 2010.

Graphic Design: Art Meets Commerce
Cover and Interior Layout: Emily Kent

ISBN–10: 1–57525–799–9
ISBN–13: 978–1–57525–799–0
10 9 8 7 6 5 4 3 2 1

TABLE OF CONTENTS

INTRODUCTION

The year 2010 marked the fortieth anniversary of Vince Lombardi's death. He died of colon cancer at Georgetown University Hospital on September 3, 1970, only eleven seasons after he had begun his incandescent run as the greatest professional football coach in history, a period during which his Green Bay Packers finished as NFL champions five times. Barely a decade of fame, yet that was all it took for him to become an American icon, the quintessential father figure coach, staring at us, pushing us, with his squat build and square jaw, his professorial glasses and camel-hair coat, his gap-toothed smile and satchelful of expressions, real and mythical, about winning and the pursuit of excellence.

All these decades after his passing, Lombardi lives on, larger than his sport, while other great coaches of his era — from George Halas to Bear Bryant to Woody Hayes — recede with time, confined to the narrow world of football. Walk into the office of an insurance salesman in Des Moines, a college financial officer in Richmond, a hockey team president in New Jersey, and there is the Lombardi credo, framed and hanging on the wall. The Lombardi bust at the Pro Football Hall of Fame in Canton has the shiniest nose, touched more than any other by the faithful, the sporting equivalent of rubbing St. Peter's foot in Rome. The ambition of every player and coach in the league is to be associated with his aura, to bask in the glow of the ultimate prize awarded to the Super Bowl champions — the Lombardi Trophy. Watch any NFL promotion on television and, inevitably, there is the profile of Lombardi, the block of granite on the sidelines.

Four decades after his passing, he was brought back to life in yet another way, striding across the Broadway stage in *Lombardi*, a new American play written by Eric Simonson. The play is said to be based on my biography, *When Pride Still Mattered*, and in a spiritual and factual sense I suppose that is true. Eric and I both come from Wisconsin. We share a similar fascination with the old coach and agree on the essential elements of the story: an exploration of the mythology of competition in American life, what it means to be a great leader, what it takes to succeed, and what it can cost. In Lombardi's case, the success was transcendent but the cost came mostly to those close to him off the playing field. He was better at creating a sense of family out of his team than he was out of his own nuclear family. That tension is at the center of Eric's play, as it was in my book. But a play is a quite different art form from a nonfiction book, and in that important way *Lombardi* is wholly original and entirely Eric's. I am proud to be associated with what he has done, distilling more than 500 pages of material into ninety powerful minutes of drama and meaning, humor and pathos.

This is a story about love, anger, fairness, frustration and perseverance. The arc of Lombardi's life, recaptured in Eric's play, follows a man who turned the traditional American success story on end. The usual tale is of a small town kid who comes to New York to make the big time. Lombardi grew up in New York, and spent the first forty-five years of his life on the East Coast. He wanted to be a head coach but never got a chance, and was about to give up, about to take a job as a banker (one of my favorite scenes in the play) before this big city kid found his way out to tiny Green Bay, a town he had visited only once before in his life, on a recruiting trip for Army football, when he had wondered how anyone could live "in this godforsaken place" — and it was there, in the smallest market in American sports, that he coached his way into history.

The man and the myth are always at play in the Lombardi story, converging and separating. Many yearn for the old man out of a longing for something they fear has been irretrievably lost. Every time a player dances and points at himself after making a routine tackle, or a mediocre athlete and his agent hold out for millions, whenever it seems that individual ego has overtaken the concept of team, people wonder, mournfully, what Lombardi would say about it. Others think Lombardi represents something less romantic, a symbol of the American obsession with winning, a philosophy that if misapplied can have unfortunate consequences in sports, business, and life. The concerns on both sides are valid, but the stereotypes from which they arise are misleading. Lombardi was more complex and interesting than the myths surrounding him. He was a figure of great talents and obvious flaws, as one of the characters in the play describes him, "the most imperfect perfect man I ever met."

David Maraniss
November 2010

AUTHOR'S NOTE

In Wisconsin, where I grew up, it's hard to get away from the "Lombardi mystique." It's in the ether there. I wasn't old enough to watch Vince Lombardi coach, but I certainly knew his story, which was the Green Bay Packer's story, and I knew his sayings, which were plastered on locker-room and boardroom walls all over the state. When David Maraniss' biography, *When Pride Still Mattered*, was published, I didn't just read it, I devoured it. The book was a revelation — the first intelligent, thoughtful, and thorough biography of a man who, up until that point, had been presented to the public in two-dimensions.

That was 1999. About the same time, I was working on a play about Frank Lloyd Wright called *Work Song*, which I directed and co-wrote with Jeffrey Hatcher. It premiered at Milwaukee Repertory Theatre, and was successful enough to get subsequent productions at theaters across the country. The experience was a good one, and I began to think about the next bio-drama. Since Milwaukee Rep had supported the first one, I thought why not attempt another Wisconsin icon?

My first pitch to Joe Hanreddy, MRT's then artistic director, was a play I called *Lombardi in Hell*, an idea loosely modeled after George Bernard Shaw's third act of *Man and Superman*. The prospective play had Vince Lombardi dreaming he had been transported to a sort of limbo where he would argue the value of winning at all costs. The cast of characters included St. Ignatius (Lombardi was schooled by Jesuits), iconic football coach Earl "Red" Blaik, John F. Kennedy and Lombardi's father, Harry. In the pitch, I described the play as a flight of fancy that might have a little something for both the football fan and the subscription audience member.

Hanreddy liked the idea, but never acted on it.

Cut to five years later: I'm on the phone with my friend and colleague Jeff Hatcher. We're talking about this and that, and he tells me that the artistic director of Madison Rep, Rick Corley, had called him about a project — the theatre was talking with David Maraniss about creating a play based on his Lombardi book, and they were looking for a writer. Jeff, known for the play *The Complete Female Stage Beauty* and for writing the films *The Duchess* and *Casanova*, said he had told Rick Corley that if he could see his way to football players dressed in 18th century garb, he might consider it. Otherwise he didn't think he was right for the job.

I begged Jeff to call Rick immediately and recommend me for the job, which he did. It took a little while to get a response, but Rick Corley eventually called me, and we started a conversation, which turned into a commission to write a play — one not too far from my original "Lombardi in Hell" idea.

That play, which Madison Rep produced in 2007 was titled *The Only Thing*. It was great experience and deserves an account all it's own. Suffice it to say, I learned a lot about writing the role of Vince Lombardi. More importantly, I made a very good friend in David Maraniss, who also became one of my favorite collaborators.

When the *Lombardi* producers Fran Kirmser and Tony Pointer approached me, at David's urging, about writing a new and different kind of play for Broadway, I didn't hesitate in saying to them that my interest in Vince Lombardi could fuel five plays. Which is true. The man is a complex prism of attributes, desires, contradictions and flaws. I also thought, "what a great idea," to put the story of Lombardi right smack dab in the middle of America's entertainment crosshairs. The man in an American icon, a hero, perhaps a tragic hero — a tragic *American* hero. His story deserves to be told; to be heard. By everyone. I've always been interested in bringing theatre to a cross-section of the public — what better subject than a man who transcended age, time, race and class?

Lombardi, this play, is a more story-driven rendering than my other Lombardi play — less fractured and metaphysical; more chronological and dramatic. Not coincidentally, the play focuses not only on Lombardi the coach, but also Lombardi the family man. This was an effort to get to his human side, and show the blemishes in a man most people associate with perfection.

And ultimately, this play fulfills for me several ambitions. One, already mentioned, is to write plays that speak not just theatre-folk — very important, I think, in a theatre world which, for most of the American population, remains mysterious and rarified.

The play also allows me the pleasure of letting my artistic side and my sports-loving side mingle and cross-pollinate. It's a unique opportunity, one that I enjoyed while working on my adaptation of *Bang the Drum Slowly*. And I don't take it for granted.

And last, but not least, I get to export a little Wisconsin heritage. Lombardi and the people who worship him, are my people, and this play has been in a big way, a thank-you card to the state that reared me.

Go Packers.

Eric Simonson
Playwright, *Lombardi*

For Sue

ACKNOWLEDGEMENTS

There are many people to thank, all of whom were essential in the development of *Lombardi*. First and foremost, David Maraniss, who wrote the quintessential book on the greatest football coach that ever lived, *When Pride Still Mattered*; not lastly, Tony Ponturo and Fran Kirmser, who had the vision to commission this play in the first place and then put it on Broadway; and also Nicole Kastrinos, who, along with Tony and Fran, shepherded the whole thing along. Special thanks to Thomas Kail, who, through his heart and generosity created the ideal creative incubator, and delivered a smashing production; to Dan Lauria, Judith Light, Keith Nobbs, Bill Dawes, Chris "Sully" Sullivan and Robert Christopher Riley who brought the play to life; to Tripp Phillips and Diane Dalton, keepers of the text; to Rick Corley, who introduced me to David Maraniss and directed my first attempt at a play about Vince Lombardi; to Stephan Dietz who read my first outline and gave me priceless feedback; to Alan Kopischke, ace proofreader and excellent sounding board; and to Susan Cremin, who read the first version of everything and offered all the support I needed during the crazy year of *Lombardi*. My son Henry works in there somewhere, probably everywhere, in small incremental ways that end in big results.

Dan Lauria stars in *Lombardi*, opening on October 21, 2010 at Broadway's Circle in the Square Theatre.

Judith Light as Marie Lombardi, Dan Lauria as Vincent Lombardi, and Keith Nobbs as Michael McCormick. Photos by Joan Marcus.

CIRCLE IN THE SQUARE

UNDER THE DIRECTION OF
THEODORE MANN and PAUL LIBIN
SUSAN FRANKEL, General Manager

Fran Kirmser Tony Ponturo

Friends of Lombardi

IN ASSOCIATION WITH
The National Football League

PRESENT

Dan Lauria Judith Light

IN

LOMBARDI

BY
Eric Simonson

BASED ON THE BOOK *When Pride Still Mattered: A Life of Vince Lombardi*
WRITTEN BY **David Maraniss**

ALSO STARRING
Keith Nobbs

Bill Dawes Robert Christopher Riley Chris Sullivan
Javon Johnson Henny Russell Brad Schmidt Jeff Still

SCENIC DESIGN **David Korins**
COSTUME DESIGN **Paul Tazewell**
LIGHTING DESIGN **Howell Binkley**
SOUND DESIGN **Acme Sound Partners**

PROJECTION DESIGN **Zachary Borovay**
HAIR DESIGN **Charles LaPointe**
DIALECT COACH **Stephen Gabis**

CASTING **Laura Stanczyk, CSA**
TECHNICAL SUPERVISOR **Peter Fulbright**
PRODUCTION STAGE MANAGER **Tripp Phillips**

PRESS REPRESENTATIVE **Boneau/Bryan-Brown**
MARKETING **HHC Marketing**
GENERAL MANAGEMENT **101 Productions, Ltd.**
EXECUTIVE PRODUCER **Red Awning**

ASSOCIATE PRODUCERS
Joseph Favorito Andrew Frank & John Mara, Jr. Rebecca Gold Al Kahn
Myla Lerner Lauren Stevens S.D. Wagner & John Johnson

DIRECTED BY
Thomas Kail

First performed at the Mahaiwe Performing Arts Center in Great Barrington, Massachusetts
The producers wish to express their appreciation to Theatre Development Fund for its support of this production.
Vince Lombardi c/o Luminary Group LLC. www.VinceLombardi.com

NOW THAT'S BROADWAY!

Bill Davis as Paul Hornung, Chris Sullivan as Jim Taylor, Robert Christopher Riley as Dave Robinson, Dan Lauria as Vincent Lombardi, Judith Light as Marie Lombardi, and Keith Nobbs as Michael McCormick. Photo by Joan Marcus.

LOMBARDI

by
Eric Simonson

CHARACTERS

Vincent Lombardi

Michael McCormick

Marie Lombardi

Paul Hornung

Dave Robinson

Jim Taylor

TIME

Mostly November, 1965; but also 1958, 1959, and 1964

PLACE

Various locations in Green Bay, WI; and Englewood, NJ

Forward slashes (/) indicate overlapped lines.

PROLOGUE

(From the darkness, a slow-motion image of a football player, struggling to free himself from the grasps of determined tacklers. We hear a crowd — a mix of cheers and boos.)

BROADCASTER VOICE #1

… We have closed the books on the nineteen-fifty-eight season, folks, and the Green Bay Packers will officially end this year with a record of one-ten-and-one, having been under-whelmed once, overwhelmed ten times, and *whelmed* once…

(As the following montage of voices dovetail one into another, we see a kaleidoscope of images which tell the story of the '58 Packers and the ascension of Vince Lombardi as their coach.)

BROADCASTER VOICE #2

The Packers, you may know, have not had a winning season in the last twelve years…

BROADCASTER VOICE #1

… A release was issued from the press office earlier today and a man named Vincent Lombardi has just been named new head coach of the Green Bay Packers…

(A light glows to reveal a familiar silhouette — camel hair coat, Homburg hat, horn-rimmed glasses: VINCE LOMBARDI. His back is slightly to us. Background sounds fade; images slow to a freeze.)

BROADCASTER VOICE #1 (CONT'D)

… the most common response from folks on the street seems to be "Lombardi. Who the heck is that?"…

(Sound cuts out; lights full on Lombardi. He proffers a football.)

LOMBARDI

Gentlemen, this is a football.

(He begins.)

This season… will be the start of something new. With every fiber of my being, I'm going to make you the best football team that I can make you. And I'll try. And I'll try again. And if I don't succeed the first time, I will try again. And you've got to give everything that is in you in order to stop the player on defense, or make the play go if you're on offense. Because this may be the one play in the whole ball game which can cause the winning or the losing of the entire season. This is a cruel and tough business. We have to produce. We're only here because we want to win and when we lose, we're gone. Therefore we have to win! Therefore you have to win! And we only want winners!

(Sound of a jet plane passing. Lights shift to MICHAEL McCORMICK, 29, slight Jersey accent. He holds a suitcase.)

MICHAEL

I'd been with *Look* Magazine less than a year and wrote about mostly minor stuff — amateur boxing, the ponies, that sort of thing. My name was so low on the magazine's masthead I was practically underwater. On one occasion, I was even sent out to Schenectady to cover a donkey basketball game. So it came as a surprise when my boss, Tom Ryder, tapped me for the Lombardi article. Fortunately, if there was one subject I knew, it was Vince Lombardi.

(Still images.)

In nineteen-fifty-eight, the Green Bay Packers were trolling the depths of professional football. In three seasons, Vince Lombardi turned those perpetual losers into perennial winners, with back-to-back championships. But then came two years of second place finishes, which for Coach Lombardi was completely unacceptable.

(Lights change.)

This year, nineteen-sixty-five, the Packers were once again poised for a championship run. Mr. Ryder had arranged special access to Mr. Lombardi's practice field, and lucky for me, I was also going to get a worm's eye view of his natural habitat.

SCENE 1

(Lights up on MARIE LOMBARDI, 40's. Her hair is done up in a bouffant. She chain smokes, speaks in a regal, Jersey accent. Right now she's poised holding a tumbler of Scotch.)

MARIE

I wasn't married to Vince Lombardi one week before I said to myself, Marie Planitz, you have made the biggest mistake of your life. I knew about his temper, his football mind-set, but at the time I thought what the hell, he's Catholic, he's stable. It'll be nice. Then, after the honeymoon, it's more like we interrupt this marriage to bring you this specially scheduled football season.

(Lights come up full on the Lombardi house-hold, Green Bay, WI — a true to form 60's ranch style home. Michael stands there listening, the same suitcase at his side.)

MICHAEL

How's it now?

MARIE

Worse. You married?

MICHAEL

No.

MARIE

Well, you ought to be, you're tall enough.

MICHAEL

I work pretty long hours.

MARIE

Married to your job?

MICHAEL

Or the job is married to me.

MARIE

Our first few years, Vin was up to his neck in coaching high school football — the Saints in Englewood, New Jersey.

MICHAEL

I went to a school in the same conference.

(Marie raises an eyebrow.)

MARIE

Don't say.

MICHAEL

St. Ignatius.

MARIE

Huh.

MICHAEL

Cecelia's was legendary.

MARIE

That's right.

MICHAEL

I followed them more closely than my alma mater, cause we weren't that great. In fact, we were pretty lousy, but the Saints. They went unbeaten for thirty-two straight games while your husband was coach.

(Marie drifts toward the front window.)

MARIE

I have a feeling you and Vince are going to get along. Look at that out there. It's black as pitch.

MICHAEL

You said he was running an errand?

MARIE

Well, sort of. One of our friends got a bit tipsy and couldn't drive himself home. After every game, we have a little party here, down in the rec room, win or lose. Mostly we win, so it's a celebration and Vince is in a pretty good mood. He's laughing, grinning from ear to ear, mixing high-balls, the whole sha-bang. Then about oh, ten or so, now, actually, he turns. Tomorrow's Monday and he has to get up for the next game, you see, in his head. And it just... takes over. Sure you don't want a drink?

MICHAEL

No, thanks.

MARIE

I should show you to your room. Just a sec, I'm due for another.

(She replenishes her drink.)

We were kind of hoping Tom would come out to do the interview. No offense.

MICHAEL

Mr. Ryder's son is on leave from Vietnam.

MARIE

I know. Tom and Vince are very good friends.

MICHAEL

That's what I understand.

MARIE

We always have a good time when he comes out for a visit.

MICHAEL

It's a very nice house you have here, Mrs. Lombardi.

MARIE

Thanks. Call me Marie. We had a two-story colonial on the other side of town the first year we were here. This is nicer.

MICHAEL

That's a lot of packing in two years.

MARIE

I actually wasn't convinced we'd be staying.

MICHAEL

Oh?

MARIE

I was in denial I guess.

(Thinks about that.)

Anyway, one more win and we clinch the conference.

MICHAEL

I know.

MARIE

(Deadpan:)

Very exciting. So. What's your article going to be about?

MICHAEL

Your husband.

MARIE

That's some article.

MICHAEL

It's not that I don't have an idea, but you never know until —

MARIE

Did you read the piece on Vince in *Esquire*? The one by that Jackass?

MICHAEL

Yes. I —

MARIE

What the hell was *that* about?

MICHAEL

It sounded to me like the guy had it out for Mr. Lombardi.

MARIE

You got that right.

MICHAEL

Pretty much a hatchet job.

MARIE

Do you know that reporter?

MICHAEL

No!

MARIE

Vince reads everything, and I mean *everything*. That one didn't sit with him too well. I was going to show you to your quarters, wasn't I?

MICHAEL

I believe so.

MARIE

Well, why didn't you say something? We thought we'd put you in our son Vincent's room. He just graduated from college. Susan — that's our daughter — is on a class trip to Washington D.C. So you and Vince will have all the privacy you need. He will be here any minute, I promise.

LOMBARDI

(Off:)

Dammit, Marie!

MARIE

Speak of the Devil.

LOMBARDI

(Off:)

What the hell are all these cigarette butts out here on the front walk?!

(Door slams off. Lombardi enters. He's in a rage.)

The front walk looks a mess again! Where's Susan?!

MARIE

(Barks back:)

In Washington D.C.!

LOMBARDI

Who the hell are you?!

MICHAEL

Michael McCormick.

MARIE

He's the reporter from New York, Vince.

LOMBARDI

(Grins.)

Ah! Tom Ryder's man.

MARIE

That's right.

LOMBARDI

Sorry there… There's a mess all over the front walk, cigarette butts.

MICHAEL

Yes, sir.

LOMBARDI

That's our daughter's job, to police that — Marie, did you offer him a drink? You're young.

MICHAEL

Young?

LOMBARDI
Younger than I expected. How old are you? Sixteen?

MICHAEL
Actually —

LOMBARDI
Marie, get me an Old Fashioned.

MARIE
Good Lord, Vincent, you want me to make you an Old Fashioned? / Now? Good Lord.

LOMBARDI
Alright, a scotch — / a scotch and soda!

MARIE
Might as well ask me to build the Taj Mahal.
(She goes to the bar.)

LOMBARDI
How old are you?

MICHAEL
Twenty-nine.

LOMBARDI
Most of the reporters I know are from New York.

MARIE
Most of the reporters you know from New York are dead.

LOMBARDI
Shut up, Marie. Red Smith is a friend of mine. You know him?

MICHAEL
Yes, sir.

LOMBARDI
Jerry Izenberg, Red Smith, Ring Lardner —

MARIE

Dead.

LOMBARDI

Tim Cohane, W.C. Hienz, you know him?

MICHAEL

Sure.

LOMBARDI

Personally?

MICHAEL

We've met.

LOMBARDI

He's a good man. Today's so called journalists?

(Waves him off.)

And don't get me started on television. Or even radio. You know Howard Cosell? That guy's got the biggest mouth east of the Mississippi, but does he say anything?

MICHAEL

Well —

LOMBARDI

Is it poetry?

MICHAEL

My dad was a reporter. He covered you when you were at St. Cecelia's.

LOMBARDI

What's his name?

MICHAEL

Pete McCormick.

LOMBARDI

You're Pete McCormick's son?

MICHAEL

Yes, sir.

LOMBARDI

I'll be dammed. He was the sports writer for the Paramus paper.

MICHAEL

The *Courier-Post*, for more than forty years. I met you a couple times way back, when I was a little kid. Your Saints were kind of a legend, and I followed your career after you left.

LOMBARDI

That right? You play? I never forget a number.

MICHAEL

Nah, I was small when I was a freshman.

LOMBARDI

Never stopped *me*.

MICHAEL

Oh, I was really small, like five foot and ninety-eight pounds small, so I sat on the sidelines and cheered. And I wrote.

(Marie hands Vince a drink.)

LOMBARDI

Marie, this fellow's dad's Pete McCormick.

MARIE

I don't know Pete McCormick.

LOMBARDI

Yes, you do.

MARIE

No, I don't.

LOMBARDI

Yes, you do.

MARIE

Okay, I do.

LOMBARDI

(Back to Michael:)

That was a decent little paper. How is your father?

MICHAEL

He passed away.

LOMBARDI

Oh.

MICHAEL

Five years ago.

LOMBARDI

I'm very sorry to hear that. It must have been a painful loss.

MICHAEL

It was. Actually… he and I'd sort of lost touch, the last couple years. Before he got sick.

LOMBARDI

That's too bad.

MICHAEL

Yeah.

(Lombardi subconsciously removes a rosary from his pocket and rolls it in his hand.)

LOMBARDI

Exceptional man. Good reporter. You come from impressive stock.

MARIE

I'm going to clean up the rec room. It looks like a bomb went off down there. Then I'm turning in so, Vin, you show him his room.

(She starts to exit.)

LOMBARDI

Didn't you?

MARIE

I never had the chance.

(She's gone.)

LOMBARDI

Sorry about that. She shoulda — well, never mind. I'm in the mood to talk. Tomorrow, who the hell knows. You feel like getting started? We beat 'em today, did you see?

MICHAEL

I was en route, on the plane.

LOMBARDI

Of course you were. We beat the pants off them.

MICHAEL

Congratulations.

LOMBARDI

And that is not necessarily a good thing.

MICHAEL

How is that not a good thing?

LOMBARDI

Sometimes we lose and if the players played with all their heart, well, then that makes me feel we are headed in the right direction. Sometimes we win and the players have not played to their potential and that's dangerous. This win, today, I know my players will take it as a sign that they are invincible and they are not. Early on this season, when we were unbeaten, everyone was saying we would go undefeated the rest of the year. Do you know how many times that has been done?

MICHAEL

Twice. The Bears both times.

LOMBARDI

That's right.

MICHAEL

Once in nineteen-thirty-four —

LOMBARDI

— That's right.

MICHAEL

— and then again in nineteen-forty-two. They went on to lose the championship both times.

LOMBARDI

And that is my point exactly! Nobody's perfect. Some of us strive for it, but nobody, nobody's perfect. This year's different. We haven't won it all since sixty-two and I want to win it all, but on the schedule of every other team in the league, there will be a circle around the date they play us because we are the team to beat. I got to find a way to get them up… but how? The entire week we spend building up an image of the enemy in our minds, until he becomes this thing we have to defeat. And then we do defeat them, we beat them handily, and it's painful for me to see the opposing coach when that happens, because I know what he's feeling. That feeling of loss, and what have I done wrong. I gotta find a way to…

(Silence.)

All that was off the record.

MICHAEL

But —

LOMBARDI

But nothing, Mister. It was off the record.

(Pause.)

You know this jerk-off from *Esquire*?

MICHAEL

I know his work.

LOMBARDI

And?

MICHAEL

People say he's the sixties' answer to Grantland Rice.

LOMBARDI

More like a donkey's answer to his back end. What about you?

MICHAEL

What?

LOMBARDI

Maybe you're the next Grantland Rice.

MICHAEL

Or maybe I'm the next Michael McCormick.

(Lombardi laughs.)

LOMBARDI

That's good. What's your piece about anyway?

MICHAEL

I want to see what it is about you that makes you win.

LOMBARDI

You should have been here two years ago when we were actually winning.

MICHAEL

You were eight, five, and one last season.

LOMBARDI

And we came in second, dammit. Had to play in that damn runners-up bowl down in Miami. Damn toilet bowl is what I call it, losers' bowl.

MICHAEL

And you lost.

LOMBARDI

(Barks:)

What the hell's the matter with you?!

MICHAEL

Sorry.

LOMBARDI

You don't think I know we lost!

MICHAEL

Sorry!

MARIE

(From the basement:)

Vince, what's going on up there?

LOMBARDI

I'm talking to Michael!

MARIE

What?!

LOMBARDI

Shut up, Marie!

MARIE

What?!

LOMBARDI

I said —

(Gives up.)

We didn't lose, we just ran out of time. But I'll be damned if we find ourselves back there again, down in second place. I'd just as soon die.

(Beat.)

We'll start tomorrow, then. You'll come to practice and see what we do, and maybe, just maybe, next week you'll see us win.

SCENE 2

(The Packer Practice Field; a crush of sound and images: Players do calisthenics, run wind sprints, charge tackle dummies. Field whistle. Lights find PAUL HORNUNG: running back, a blonde Adonis — standing next to DAVE "ROBBIE" ROBINSON: big, African-American, Outside Linebacker. Both are in practice gear; both are winded.)

ROBINSON

Sonofabitch is going to kill us before the week's out. You'd hardly know we just won that last game thirty-five to zip.

HORNUNG

He's riding you hard today, Robbie.

ROBINSON

Not like I don't deserve it.

HORNUNG

You look okay to me out there.

ROBINSON

Last drill, I'm not breaking hard enough off the snap on the blitz. I got the left side down pretty good, but the right side's busting my ass.

HORNUNG

I'm gonna get myself an ice cube. You want one?

ROBINSON

Are you crazy? Coach would kill us.

HORNUNG

But I'm thirsty.

ROBINSON

Your funeral, Pal.

(Paul trots off. Crash of pads as lights shift to Michael, in his hat and coat. He talks to us.)

MICHAEL

The Packers' practice field was a flat worn-out plane on the outskirts of Green Bay. Gray sky forever, dotted every now and then by smoke stack or simple white house. If the Packers were winning, maybe it was because there was absolutely nothing else to do around here.

(Lights shift to Lombardi in a cap and practice jacket.)

LOMBARDI

Come on, hit him, Hawg! Hit him! Make it hurt! Dammit, what the hell's the matter with you, Nitschke?! You got a lot of dog in you, I tell you! You're dogs I tell you! Paul, Robbie, let's move. *A bunch of dogs! For the love of Pete! Thurston, you're fat!* What are you gonna do about number fifty-one? He's fast, dammit! He's fast. *You're fat!*

(Whistle. Lights shift to JIM TAYLOR: a muscular fullback. He stands apart, hunched over, trying to catch his breath. Michael approaches.)

MICHAEL

Hey. Mike McCormick, *Look* Magazine. You're Jim Taylor.

TAYLOR

Beat it.

MICHAEL

You think you'll hit a thousand yards again this year?

TAYLOR

Beat it, Roy.

(Robinson enters up, looks on.)

MICHAEL

Um, Mike, from *Look* Magazine. Is this a good time to talk?

ROBINSON

(Approaching.)

Hey.

MICHAEL

I just need five minutes. I'm doing a story on —

ROBINSON

Hey, Man.

MICHAEL

— on Coach Lombardi, and I thought you might have a few —

ROBINSON

I'm talking to you.

MICHAEL

I — Hi, I just have some questions —

ROBINSON

How the hell'd you get past the ropes?

MICHAEL

I'm from *Look* Magazine.

ROBINSON

I don't care where you're from, Pal. No reporters supposed to be this side of the ropes, or are you lost?

MICHAEL

You're Dave Robinson.

ROBINSON

Yeah, I know who I am. Come on Jim, let's go inside before we're missed.

TAYLOR

I can handle myself, Rookie.

ROBINSON

I ain't no rookie.

TAYLOR

Barely you're not. Barely you're not a rookie.

MICHAEL

(To Robinson:)

You're a third year man out of Penn State. All American — nineteen-sixty-two…

ROBINSON

Will you shut the hell up. What do you think this is, an honor's banquet?

TAYLOR

And just because you're Players' Representative don't mean you got a spot forever on this team.

ROBINSON

Okay, I get it.

TAYLOR

You're gonna find yourself on board a bus bound for some AFL expansion team or something like that.

MICHAEL

Is there going to be a trade?

ROBINSON/TAYLOR

No!

ROBINSON

Jim, you want to talk about the Players' Association, you can get me anytime after practice.

TAYLOR

Don't think I won't.

ROBINSON

Okay.

TAYLOR

Okay.

(To Michael:)

And you.

(Walks past Robinson and hovers over Michael.)

Stay the hell away from me. You fellas got me in trouble once and I got no desire to get into it again.

LOMBARDI

(Off:)

Taylor!

TAYLOR

(Under his breath:)

Goddammit!

LOMBARDI

(Off:)

Robinson!

ROBINSON

See what you caused?

TAYLOR

You're the one who caused it, Rookie. If you hadn't come over here, it wouldn't've looked like a goddam convention.

(Lombardi enters.)

LOMBARDI

Jim, two trips around the goal post. Now!

TAYLOR

Coach —

LOMBARDI

Don't argue with me! Do it!

(Jim runs off, but not without first glaring at Michael.)

Dave, get inside with the rest of the defense before I do you the same favor I just did Jim.

(Slaps him on the back. Robinson starts to exit.)

Dave.

ROBINSON

(Stops.)

Yes, Coach?

LOMBARDI

Watch getting off your right side on the snap.

ROBINSON

I know, Coach.

LOMBARDI

You get caught flat-footed every time.

ROBINSON

I'm trying my best.

LOMBARDI

Not good enough.

ROBINSON

Thanks, Coach.

LOMBARDI

I'm watching you, Robbie. Go.

(Robinson exits.)

MICHAEL

That wasn't Taylor's fault, Coach. I —

LOMBARDI

Listen to me. Do not go talking to Jim Taylor. He cannot handle himself in front of reporters.

MICHAEL

But you've got to let me talk to your players.

LOMBARDI

I do not have to do anything, Mister! You are my guest.

MICHAEL

Can I just —

LOMBARDI

Do you want to remain on this side of the ropes?

MICHAEL

Yes, sir.

LOMBARDI

Okay. The players sometimes have a habit of letting reporters know certain things they should not know about, injuries and such, and I am not interested in giving my opponents ammunition they can use to beat us. Do you understand? Now, Jim Taylor — he's a work horse and one hell of a ball player, but he's not so smart when it comes to speaking his mind.

(Looks off, grins broadly.)

Paul!

(Back to Michael:)

Let me tell you something about Paul Hornung. That man is an average running back at best, but get him inside the twenty and he is unstoppable. Really.
Paul! Come over here!
One of the greatest players of all time, an immortal. You talk to Paul Hornung.

(Hornung enters.)

HORNUNG

Hiya, Coach.

LOMBARDI

Paul, I — What's that you got in your mouth? Chewing gum?

HORNUNG

Just an ice cube, Coach.

LOMBARDI

Well, spit it out, dammit. Do you want to get your damn tongue bitten off?

HORNUNG

No.

LOMBARDI

Spit it out.

HORNUNG

Swallowed it.

LOMBARDI

I told you to spit it out!

HORNUNG

Sorry, Coach.

LOMBARDI

And wipe that smile off your face.

(He does.)

Paul, talk to this reporter. He's one of the real boys, from New York.

(Whistle blows.)

See you inside. How to go out there, Paul, how to hustle!

(Lombardi leaves.)

HORNUNG

Listen, Mister, I don't mind talking, but I also got a date with the trainer like, right now. My knee cap's just about to jump right out of my skin. And after that I got a date with a former Miss Teen USA, so —

MICHAEL

Paul Hornung.

HORNUNG

Yes, sir?

MICHAEL

The Golden Boy.

HORNUNG

Aw, around here most of the boys just call me Horn or Goat.

MICHAEL

I saw Notre Dame play Navy your junior year. You were amazing.

HORNUNG

Thanks, Pal.

MICHAEL

You looked pretty good out there this morning, too.

HORNUNG

Still not a hundred percent.

MICHAEL

Must have been tough. I mean, after the year off.

HORNUNG

Hell, everything's tough at my age, and it's hard, you know, sitting on the bench wasting away with injuries. After a while people start to talk. Ain't that right, Mr. Reporter?

MICHAEL

Mike.

HORNUNG

Oh — okay. Mike. This game, though, I can feel it. This game's gonna turn things around for me. Catch you later.

(He exits. Lights shift: a film projector whirls to life. Lombardi gets into position to address his Players.)

MICHAEL

(To us:)

Each morning after a workout, the players trotted back to a plain tan brick building for chalk talk.

LOMBARDI

Gentlemen, we had a terrific game on Sunday and I do not want to take that away from you, but if you think we were flawless, well, then you've got another think coming.

MICHAEL

The rest of the first day went more or less the same. Every player I talked to pretty much grunted yes and no answers.

LOMBARDI

Wait, wait, roll that back. You see that, Robbie?

MICHAEL

I wasn't getting much.

LOMBARDI

How many times do I have to tell you to square off before you tackle the guy? Square off, then tackle.

MICHAEL

(Taking out a ten-cent notebook.)

And Lombardi? I couldn't get him to sit down for more than two minutes.

LOMBARDI

That mistake, Robbie, lives on in the life of this footage to the end of all time. You have a chance, however, to pay penance for your sins out there on the playing field.

MICHAEL

(Paging through notebook.)

I try not to use a notepad during interviews, and then I jot down what I remember after.

LOMBARDI

Alright, let's get to the interception.

MICHAEL

Something I learned from my dad. Makes the subject feel less observed, less —

LOMBARDI

Good grab there, Willie! But where the hell is Davis on the return?!

MICHAEL

(Reading:)

Okay, this is from Wednesday, three whole days after I'd arrived: "Born in Brooklyn, oldest of five, two brothers, two sisters."

LOMBARDI

When we go out on that field again, we are going to run that tip drill until we get it right!

MICHAEL

"Father a butcher, whacked us from time to time."

LOMBARDI
That's it, boys. We're done for the day.

MICHAEL
"Graduated from Fordham. Mother a perfectionist." Nothing but Pulitzer material here. My big break and I was blowing it. First I panicked, then I got an idea.

SCENE 3

(The Lombardi home, late afternoon.)

MARIE
One olive or two? Three if you like, make it dirty.

MICHAEL
Two will do me, thanks.

MARIE
Teetotaler, you. I was beginning to think maybe you were on the wagon.

MICHAEL
I'm not that great at holding my alcohol.

MARIE
A man your size?

MICHAEL
I got endless kidding in college. It doesn't sit well in the press corps either.

MARIE
I can imagine.

MICHAEL
Every story ends at Toots Shor's. You know that bar?

MARIE

Vince and I practically lived there when we were in Jersey. You're making me homesick.

(Puts in the olives.)

The Rainbow Room uses onions. You ever heard of that? I don't know if I like it much. Do you have any idea what a pimento is?

MICHAEL

None.

MARIE

Neither do I, but it's got to be in one of the four food groups, right?

(Hands him his drink.)

MICHAEL

Sure.

MARIE

(Raises her glass.)

Well, then. To nutrition.

(They drink.)

Vince is a hard nut, especially in the middle of the season. Anything that hasn't got to do with his Packers...

MICHAEL

Right.

MARIE

There's no brain space for it. He hasn't remembered our anniversary in twenty-two years. He's hardly ever in the mood for a chat. Paul's got a lot of great stories.

MICHAEL

He didn't seem too interested in opening up.

MARIE

Of course not. He doesn't know you.

MICHAEL

Anyway, the one I'd really like to talk to is Jim Taylor.

MARIE

He's off limits, right?

MICHAEL

Yeah, and I don't get it.

MARIE

There's nothing — /

MICHAEL

He can hand — / Sorry.

MARIE

Nevermind.

MICHAEL

It's just that the guy can handle himself. He's not a ten year-old, you know? And I got a feeling —

MARIE

Michael.

MICHAEL

It's only a feeling, but I think there's still waters there —

MARIE

Michael.

MICHAEL

What?

MARIE

You're giving me a headache.

MICHAEL

Sorry.

MARIE

You're a very excitable young man.

MICHAEL

Sorry, Mrs. Lombardi.

MARIE

Stop apologizing. And call me Marie. Sit.

(He does.)

You want Jim because you can't have him. But trust me, there's not much there. Vince needs him, he's talented. That's about it.

MICHAEL

He calls me Roy.

MARIE

He calls everybody Roy. He can't remember anybody's name.

MICHAEL

Oh.

MARIE

There're rumors he's not going to re-sign with the Packers next year. This game coming up, it's important to him — you know, nationally televised, etcetera, etcetera. He's probably not going to be in the mood to talk. Forget Jim. Go after Paul.

MICHAEL

Right.

MARIE

Now: Vince. Two things.

MICHAEL

Shoot.

MARIE

One. God, family and the Green Bay Packers are the three most important things in his life. But not necessarily in that order. In fact, I'd put his family a distant third and God doesn't rank number one, so.

MICHAEL

Oh.

MARIE

Though to Vince's credit, he never misses a morning mass.

MICHAEL

What's number two?

MARIE

He loves his players. And I don't mean he just likes them an awful lot. He truly, actually, loves them.

MICHAEL

He has a strange way of showing it.

MARIE

Yes, he is a man of extremes. Most people see only the rage, you know, the anger.

MICHAEL

All in the name of football, huh?

MARIE

Football's just what he happens to be doing. Could be anything, he'd be just as…

MICHAEL

Obsessive?

MARIE

Focused. There was a time, I actually thought he might get out of football altogether. Right before we came here.

MICHAEL

When he was coaching the Giants?

MARIE

Assistant coaching. Big, big difference.

MICHAEL

He was frustrated.

MARIE

Beyond frustrated.

MICHAEL

What else on Earth would he possibly do?

MARIE

Banker.

MICHAEL

No.

MARIE

Swear to God.

MICHAEL

Vince Lombardi?

MARIE

I know. Can you imagine.

MICHAEL

(As Vince:)

You want a loan?! *You think you deserve a loan?!*

(Beat.)

Sorry.

MARIE

Funny. But really. He worked at a bank in Jersey during the off-season.

MICHAEL

I didn't know that.

MARIE

Hardly anybody did, but that last year he got this idea in his head...

SCENE 4

(Lights up on Lombardi. Frank Sinatra sings a holiday tune from a Hi-Fi.)

LOMBARDI

... Why not make it a full-time deal? I figure you can run a bank just the same way you run a football team. So I am making it my business to know all the positions.

(Lights expand to reveal Lombardi's New Jersey home, 1958. Marie steps into the scene, trades a fresh highball for Vince's winter gear.)

MARIE

Sure.

LOMBARDI

Bank teller, she's the receiver, I guess. Security guard, the offensive lineman, protecting the quarterback, who's the bank manager. All the positions, all the way down to janitor. He'd be the grounds crew, something like that.

MARIE

You got a call today.

LOMBARDI

Wait, I'm talking.

MARIE

Sorry.

LOMBARDI

I've got something — Cheers —

(He lifts his glass; she lifts hers.)

Something I want to tell you. The bank president called me into his office. Said he'd like to make me an executive, maybe as soon as March.

MARIE

Which would — He said what?

LOMBARDI

It means I would quit football altogether.

(Marie thinks about this.)

MARIE

Uh-huh.

LOMBARDI

Why are you looking at me like that?

MARIE

I'm not saying anything.

LOMBARDI

But you're thinking it.

MARIE

No.

LOMBARDI

What?

MARIE

It's just I'd like to see you halfway through next season when you're sitting at home watching the Giants on TV.

LOMBARDI

The folks at the bank are nice!

MARIE

Vince, settle down.

LOMBARDI

They lead normal lives. I'd get up in the morning, I'd come home at a decent hour. I thought you'd like that.

MARIE

I would like that.

LOMBARDI

You know I get these horrible stomach pains all season long.

MARIE

Mm-hm.

LOMBARDI

It's a crazy game, that's what I decided.

MARIE

This again.

LOMBARDI

What's that supposed to mean?

MARIE

I don't know, we get the same speech, every year. It's a crazy game.

LOMBARDI

Every time I step away from it, I get a perspective on it, Marie.

MARIE

I want a normal life, Vince, but I don't want you to be miserable.

LOMBARDI

Then you don't know me.

MARIE

You get in a state, especially after the last game of the season. As the days get shorter, your mood —

LOMBARDI

Marie, / you don't have to tell me!

MARIE

Your mood grows darker. / Vince!

LOMBARDI

I'm talking!

(She shuts up. He sighs.)

Would you put that on the rocks, please?

(Marie takes his glass, goes to refresh it while Lombardi settles.)

They have been playing football for nearly a hundred years. Marie?

MARIE

I'm listening. Keep talking.

LOMBARDI

I don't think there's one new play, formation, *thing* that hasn't been invented somewhere by somebody. What more can I add to the equation? Hell, in another year, my playbook will be down to a couple pages only.

MARIE

And what would it say?

(Hands him his re-fill. She settles next to him.)

LOMBARDI

One page would say blocking and the other tackling. Blocking and tackling, that's all it is.

MARIE

And yet it requires human beings with human emotions.

LOMBARDI

Agreed. It has become a game for madmen.

MARIE

You got no argument from me.

LOMBARDI

(Looks at her.)

So. You want to be the wife of a banker?

MARIE

What do you want, Vince?

LOMBARDI

Don't throw it back on me like that.

MARIE

What? Do what you want, because it's all going to boil down to that in the end.

LOMBARDI

I'm asking your advice.

MARIE

Then I am telling you that if you want this bank job, you should take it and never look back.

LOMBARDI

Get out of football.

MARIE

Yes. But whatever you decide, if it doesn't go well, I don't want you to blame me. As long as I've known you, Vince, you haven't strayed more than two feet from a football field.

LOMBARDI

So you don't want me to take the job.

MARIE

No.

LOMBARDI

Then what do you want me to do?!

MARIE

I want *you* to make the decision.

LOMBARDI

(Restless now.)

Dammit! In fifteen years, I have never been offered a head coaching job at a college *or* professional level. In spite of the fact that I've been a part of only winning traditions!

MARIE

Vince.

LOMBARDI

Hell, I got all those years under Red Blaik at Army. Only winning seasons at the Giants the last five years. We nearly won it all this past season! Everyone tells me I should have been a head coach by now. And nothing. Why? And the only thing I can think of is that my last name ends in a vowel.

MARIE

Vince!

LOMBARDI

What?

MARIE

Are you finished?

LOMBARDI

Yes.

MARIE

Jack Vainisi called today.

LOMBARDI

Huh?

MARIE

Jack Vainisi phoned for you. You were at the bank —

LOMBARDI

The — ah — he's with the Packers.

MARIE

That's right.

LOMBARDI

Their personnel man, and he's good. Shame he works for Green Bay.

MARIE

He's conducting —

LOMBARDI

Waste of talent if you ask me. Sorry Marie, what?

MARIE

He can tell you himself.

(Handing a slip of paper.)

He wants you to call him as soon as possible.

(Vince dials; Marie starts off.)

LOMBARDI

The Giants were trying to get Jack away from Green Bay a couple years ago, but he was stuck in a contract — Where are you going?

MARIE

To get an atlas.

(She exits.)

LOMBARDI

Everyone in the league knows he's one of the best scouts — and he's Italian! He found Max McGee playing on an Air Force base down in Texas, brought him up —

(On the phone:)

Jack, hi, Vince Lombardi... Same to you. Happy New Year. How're things up in Green Bay?...

(Laughs.)

I won't any tell any tales out of school... So what's up?

(Long listen.)

That's... No, that's very interesting. Can I get back to you?... How about tomorrow?...

(Marie re-enters with a huge Rand-McNally atlas.)

Okay, thanks… Yeah-yeah, Jack. Bye.

(Hangs up.)

What's that for?

(She sets the book down and pages through.)

MARIE

I'm going to find Green Bay. I have no idea where it is. Do you know?

LOMBARDI

Wisconsin.

MARIE

Where is *that*?

LOMBARDI

West of here. I'm not about to take a coaching job in Green Bay.

MARIE

Mm-hm.

LOMBARDI

Hell, I don't even know that conference. Anyway, no one's offered the job. They're just doing a preliminary search. And they got this damn search committee. It's a community-owned team, no owner.

MARIE

G, R, E.

LOMBARDI

Jack wanted to know if I would throw my hat into the ring.

MARIE

Did you tell him you were sorry, that you were a banker now?

LOMBARDI

No.

MARIE

(After a beat, back to the atlas:)

Green Bay. Page one-fourteen. D, six.

LOMBARDI

(Paces.)

It'd take years to rebuild. They got that Hornung fellow. Ray Nitschke, Jim Ringo. Chocked full of talent, and no direction.

(Lombardi's mind is racing.)

That team hasn't done well for nearly a decade. Nowhere to go but up. Jack says it's the coaching job *and* general manager.

MARIE

I can't find it anywhere.

LOMBARDI

Dammit, Marie, I want it! I want it, damn it!

(He goes to the phone, dials.)

MARIE

What about the bank?

LOMBARDI

The bank can wait.

MARIE

(Back to the atlas:)

Oshkosh, Sheboygan, Kewaunee. Is it an Indian reservation?

LOMBARDI

Thing I have to worry about is that their board won't get in the way — Hello, Jack. Vince… No, I wanted to tell you I don't have to think about it. I'm in. What do I need to do? … Okay… Okay, bye.

(Goes to Marie, grabs her.)

I got a good feeling about this, Marie. I think this is gonna be it.

MARIE

What did Jack say?

LOMBARDI

I need to sit tight. Let him do some leg-work, grease the wheels. I got to — I got to get to work. Study up on the Green Bay Packehs.

(He bends down, kisses her.)

Marie, this is gonna be great.

(He starts to exit. She pulls him back.)

MARIE

I love you, Vince.

LOMBARDI

I love you too, Rie.

(He looks at the atlas, points.)

Right there. Bottom of the Bay.

(He exits. Marie stares at the map.)

SCENE 5

(Lights shift back to Michael and Marie at the Lombardi house. Marie looks over the same atlas.)

MARIE

Bottom of the Bay.

(She traces the path she describes.)

The day we drove out here from Jersey, it was February, and there'd been a blizzard the night before. We rounded Lake Michigan and passed Chicago and then, all of the sudden, white. Nothing, as far as the eye could see. No one spoke for hours. Where is he taking us, I thought, me and the kids. And I started to cry.

(Turns to Michael.)

Please don't put that in your article, Michael. The folks around here already think I'm a snob.

MICHAEL

Okay.

MARIE

I do miss New York. I miss going to Bloomingdale's, the Met. I miss sopping — shopping — for nice shoes…

MICHAEL

Your husband's done well here.

MARIE

Yes. He has become a very famous person. You know, when we're walking through airports, sometimes I purposely stay several steps behind Vince, just to watch people stop and stare as he walks by.

(She closes the atlas.)

Everyone knows me here. That, I appreciate. Will you turn out the lights?

MICHAEL

Can I — I thought I might get in touch with your son.

MARIE

Why on earth for?

MICHAEL

Just to talk. You know, for background.

(She advances.)

MARIE

Listen, Mister, you can use the stuff I told you, and if I end up coming off bad, well, what Vince gives, I can take, but keep my son out of this. God knows he had enough of Vin while he was growing up, enough of the back of his hand. He ought to get out of his father's shadow once and for all.

(She stops herself, on the verge of tears. Door opens off. Marie backs away.)

LOMBARDI

(Off:)

Marie!

MARIE

Jesus. I should learn to keep my mouth shut.

(Lombardi walks in.)

LOMBARDI

Marie — Bart Starr is injured.

(Hands her his coat.)

MARIE

How?

LOMBARDI

Torn ligament. Marie, I got to get some sleep.

MARIE

God, your hands are cold. You should stand by the heater.

(Lombardi moves to Michael.)

LOMBARDI
Michael, where in the hell did you go today? You're supposed to be watching!

MARIE
Don't yell at him, Vin.

LOMBARDI
I was just asking him a question. Where were you?

MARIE
It's very late and you're being very loud.

LOMBARDI
I'm talking in a normal voice, Rie.

MARIE
You never talk in a normal voice.

LOMBARDI
Don't start with me on that.

MARIE
This is not the way you treat a guest.

LOMBARDI
He —

MARIE
Listen! We were having a conversation, while you were at practice.

LOMBARDI
He's supposed to be writing an article!

MARIE
And he will!

MICHAEL
It's alright, Mrs. Lombardi.

LOMBARDI
What were you two talking about?

MARIE

Vince —

MICHAEL

It's my fault, Coach Lombardi —

MARIE

Michael, I can handle this. Vince, I'm allowed to have a conversation —

LOMBARDI

No no no no no, what the hell were you two talking about?

MARIE

(Barks.)

I can talk to whomever I want when I want and I don't need your permission so back off!

(Vince stands there a moment.)

LOMBARDI

Jeez, Rie.

MARIE

… I told him about when the call came from the Packers.

LOMBARDI

Oh. Ancient history.

MICHAEL

Will — um… will Starr be able to play on Sunday?

LOMBARDI

We don't know. Don't go telling your reporter friends.

MICHAEL

Okay.

LOMBARDI

You know, I had our press guy get me some of your articles. You're good.

MICHAEL

Thanks.

LOMBARDI

Don't let it go to your head. Good night.

(Lombardi buckles over in pain.)

Ah!

MARIE

Vince!

(Marie goes to him.)

LOMBARDI

That one hurt.

MARIE

He's been having stomach problems.

MICHAEL

Should I call someone?

LOMBARDI

No! No... Nothing a little Pepto-Bismol won't fix.

MARIE

He won't get tested.

LOMBARDI

You wouldn't either if the doctor was trying to shove a big snake up your ass.

(Beat.)

Medical procedure.

MICHAEL

Oh.

(They wait.)

LOMBARDI

I'm okay. It's gone now... Rie, I'm sorry I yelled at you.

MARIE

I know. Me too.

LOMBARDI

I… I'm gonna turn in.

(He exits.)

MARIE

Good night, Michael.

MICHAEL

Good night, Mrs. Lombardi.

(Beat. She looks at him.)

Marie.

(She leaves. Michael speaks to us:)

The next morning, Friday, I went to the practice field and was surprised when Paul Hornung pulled me aside and wanted to talk.

SCENE 6

(Lights shift to the practice field locker room. Paul Hornung, in practice gear, sits on a training table holding an ice pack on his knee.)

HORNUNG

The thing I've got to watch out for is this right knee. I keep thinking it's all a result of that damn year I lost. As you know, I ran into a bit of trouble and they suspended me.

MICHAEL

I know.

HORNUNG

Yeah, I guess everyone knows, and that's what you get when you hang around with the wrong bunch of fellows. All I can say is, I'm glad Coach Lombardi asked me back. I was clean all last year and the year before — not the injuries, but the partying. Mostly. Coach told me to stay at the foot of the cross.

MICHAEL

But a drink every now and then…

HORNUNG

(Smiles.)

A man's got needs. Marie Lombardi's always after me to find a nice girl and settle down. But, hell, why get married in the morning when you never know who you'll meet that night?

(Tries to stand.)

Goddammit, that hurts. I wish it was Monday. God knows I need the rest.

MICHAEL

So does Bart.

HORNUNG

How'd you hear about him?

MICHAEL

Coach told me.

HORNUNG

He never lets anyone in on the injury report.

MICHAEL

It was late.

HORNUNG

(Looks at him.)

Marie called me this morning. Said you were all right.

MICHAEL

She told me if I wanted to get to the real Lombardi, I had to talk to Paul Hornung.

HORNUNG

Oh, I don't know about that.

MICHAEL

You were already here, his first season.

HORNUNG

Yeah, fifty-nine. Before that, I was about ready to quit football all together.

MICHAEL

That bad?

HORNUNG

Not if you wanted to slack off. And I did for a while, but then you get sick of the game — not the game of football, but trying to get away with stuff. It's a hell of a lot of work.

(Beat.)

You wanna know something about Coach, something that so far no newspaper man's ever picked up on?

MICHAEL

I'm all ears.

HORNUNG

His voice.

MICHAEL

Okay.

HORNUNG

One time, we were doing calisthenics. And there was this dog, this little terrier or something. I don't know whose it was, but he was barking up a storm and going in and out of our legs while we were doing jumping jacks and all, and we're all yelling at the dog to get out of the way. Jim Taylor even kicks it a distance but nothing keeps it from yapping. All of the sudden, Coach Lombardi comes down from the offices. He takes a good long look around, sees what's going on and yells *Who let that dog on the field!* And it shuts up. Just like that. Coach yells again *Get that mutt the hell off my practice field!* And no lie, this dog skedaddles out of sight faster than poop through a goose. The entire press corps are laughing and laughing, and Coach just looks around like, What just happened? He had no idea.

LOMBARDI

(Entering:)

Gentlemen!

HORNUNG

You ever listen to him talk?

LOMBARDI

Give me your attention.

HORNUNG

That voice could raise the dead.

(Lights shift to Lombardi, addressing his Players.)

LOMBARDI

All of you know that this is my first season here in Green Bay. One thing about the Packers: it's a team with a great tradition and that tradition has been developed through one thing only and that's pride. Now. How do you develop pride? Pride is developed by a winning tradition. I'm only here because I want to win. Actually the only difference between any one player in this league, any one *team* in the league, is an *energy*. This is a cruel game. Therefore, you have got to give everything that is in you, you have got to keep yourself in prime physical condition because fatigue will make cowards of us all. Now, I have never — never — been a part of a losing tradition and I do not intend to start now. From here on in you will talk like, you will look like, and you will act like the most dignified professionals in your hometown, for the goal here is to make the Green Bay Packers the Yankees of professional football and anyone who doesn't like it is perfectly free to get the hell out. Right now! There are trains, planes and buses leaving here every day, and if you don't produce for me you're gonna find yourself on one of them!

SCENE 7

(Lombardi's office, 1959; Lombardi, followed by Hornung and Taylor, both in street clothes.)

LOMBARDI

Come in, boys.

HORNUNG

Hello, Coach —

(Taylor grunts.)

LOMBARDI

How'd I do out there, fellas?

HORNUNG

Well, I tell you Mr. Lombardi, you got their attention.

LOMBARDI

They could have walked out at once for all I knew. Paul, we spoke over the phone. A couple months ago. Just a second. Jim Taylor.

TAYLOR

Sir?

LOMBARDI

I'm glad to finally meet you. But I did not expect either of you until three days from now.

HORNUNG

Yes, sir.

LOMBARDI

Was there some sort of confusion with the dates? You're here early.

HORNUNG

Just a day or two.

LOMBARDI

Three days! How come?! This camp right now is for rookies and invites only. What the hell are you hanging around camp for?!

HORNUNG

Well sir —

LOMBARDI

That is not a question, Mister! If you come around camp, you come to work out, not to stand around and watch, or sit with the others during lunch to make conversation. That is what we call a distraction. Why are you here?!

(He waits.)

That's actually a real question. Answer.

HORNUNG

Me and a couple of the boys, we were...

LOMBARDI

What?! You were what?!

HORNUNG

Nothing.

LOMBARDI

Were you thinking you could get a head start on your bar hopping?

HORNUNG

No, sir.

LOMBARDI

Do not lie to me, Paul Hornung! You were spotted until all hours of the night at a place called Bucky's Beanery. This establishment is now off limits. I've got a list —

(Picks up a piece of paper from his desk.)

I've got a list here —

(Paul approaches to get a better look.)

Get out! I've got a list here of all the bars and restaurants you are never, ever allowed to frequent again, and if I catch you there, you will be fined. Do you understand?

HORNUNG

Yes, sir.

LOMBARDI

Jim Taylor, why are you here early?

TAYLOR

I messed up on my calendar dates.

LOMBARDI

(After a moment:)

Both of you owe me fifty dollars.

TAYLOR

What for?!

LOMBARDI

You missed curfew.

TAYLOR

I didn't go out drinking.

LOMBARDI

Yet you weren't in your bed by ten o'clock.

HORNUNG

I thought curfew didn't start till Tuesday.

LOMBARDI

Mister, curfew started the day you showed up to camp! There is going to be a new way of doing things around here. Do you understand?

TAYLOR/HORNUNG

Yes, sir.

LOMBARDI

Now — While I got you here, we might as well make it worth our time. Tomorrow, you two are going to suit up and work out with the rest of the team. Jim Taylor, you are my starting fullback. That is not going to change. Paul Hornung, the previous coach had you playing practically every position on the field.

HORNUNG

Yes, sir.

LOMBARDI

From quarterback to running back and place kicker. Safety, punt and kick-off returns.

HORNUNG

Yup.

LOMBARDI

How do you feel about that?

HORNUNG

When you put it that way, Coach, it makes me feel kind of tired.

LOMBARDI

Of course it does, because you can't do it. Nobody can. Did you like losing?

HORNUNG

Nobody likes losing.

LOMBARDI

That is my point exactly. I want you to know one thing, Paul Hornung, you won't have to worry about playing five positions anymore. You are my left halfback. You are my Frank Gifford. You're either going to make it as my left halfback or you're not going to make it in pro football. You understand?

HORNUNG

Yes, sir.

LOMBARDI

Gentlemen: every team has a certain play that is theirs and if they are good enough at running it, then there is no team that can stop it. Ours is the Power Sweep, we call it forty-eight, and you two are the cornerstones of that play. Jim, you and Paul here are my thunder and lightning — the engine that drives this team to victory!

(Goes to the chalk board, writes. Now he is speaking to the entire team.)

And this, Gentlemen, will be our bread-and-butter play.

(Diagrams the play. Film and still images wash over the set.)

The tight end — open wide exactly nine feet from the tackle. The guard, Jerry Kramer, is a little wider than usual, with more latitude to pull left or right. That's you, Thurston — you may break the play inside *or* outside, depending on how the play has broken. We will create a seal *here* and a seal *here,* and Paul Hornung or Jim Taylor, as soon as you get the ball, you will follow the blocker, and run, in. The. *Alley! Run to daylight!* Wherever it shows. *Inside* the defensive end, *inside* the defensive tackle, *outside* the defensive line-backer. R*un to daylight.* Forty-eight. Now, gentlemen, this play can break any one of those three places. But ultimately, on this one play, we have a hundred different options. Each man must read the defense as it happens and block according to his own discretion. It is the team that decides which way this play will go, each player making split second decisions in concert. This is our signature play. This is the play that we must make go. Every team in the league is going to know we're going to run this play, and no matter how hard they try to stop us, they won't. Because they can't! And we will run it again, and again, and again!

(Lights shift back to Hornung and Michael.)

HORNUNG

That season we went from one-ten-and-one to seven-and-five. Freedom through discipline. Eleven men, one mind.

MICHAEL

Freedom through discipline — that's a Jesuit principle.

HORNUNG

Hell, I don't know. Just something I hear Coach Lombardi say all the time.

MICHAEL

What else?

HORNUNG

What else what?

MICHAEL

You guys aren't winning because of just one play.

HORNUNG

No — well, maybe we are. All I know is we were losing before Coach came, and we're winning now.

SCENE 8

(Lights shift to the Lombardi house — Michael and Marie.)

MARIE

If I never hear the number forty-eight again — but Paul's right, that play's Vince's gospel, the beginning and the end. What else did he tell you?

MICHAEL

That the players come to you whenever they feel Coach is riding them too hard.

MARIE

Paul told you that?

MICHAEL

He said you're the only person who can talk him into letting up.

MARIE

You know, I'm gonna have a word with Paul the next time I see him.

MICHAEL

I don't want to get him into trouble.

MARIE

He's never out of trouble.

MICHAEL

Is it true, what Paul said?

MARIE

No comment.

(Doorbell rings.)

There's my ride.

(Presents herself.)

How do I look?

MICHAEL

Pretty great.

MARIE

I never thought turquoise was my color, but the sales lady at Prange's talked me into it.

MICHAEL

Where are you going?

MARIE

I'm in charge of a Players' Wives function tonight. A few of the girls and I are going out for a little high ball before-hand. Would you like to join us, Michael? They might have some interesting insight on Vince Lombardi.

MICHAEL

Okay.

MARIE

I'm joking. Get your butt back to the practice field.

MICHAEL

Right.

MARIE

You have a golden opportunity here and only two days left till Sunday.

SCENE 9

(Lights up on the Practice field. Lombardi stands on the sidelines. We can hear the players practice off a distance.)

LOMBARDI

(Sudden pain in the stomach.)

Ah!

(Buckles over.)

Christ almighty.

(Michael approaches.)

MICHAEL

How we doing?

LOMBARDI

Jordan's got the flu, that's a new one. And then there's Starr.

MICHAEL

I meant you.

LOMBARDI

What about me?

MICHAEL

Your stomach.

LOMBARDI

My cross to bear.

MICHAEL

You should probably have that —

LOMBARDI

You know, I never taught English at St. Cecelia's, but I do know good writing from bad. A lot of these journalists today are sloppy, they disregard the basic rules of English and it bugs the crap out of me. We had this documentary crew here last year, they were putting together a film of one of our winter games and the narration kept referring to the field as this frozen tundra. Lambeau Field, the *frozen tundra.* Do you believe it?

MICHAEL

What's wrong with that?

LOMBARDI

It's redundant, dammit! If it's a tundra, it's already frozen.

MICHAEL

Oh.

LOMBARDI

Point is, you've got good language skills.

MICHAEL

Some of the new writers are trying something different.

LOMBARDI

(Waves his hand.)

All crap, all self-serving garbage. You've got to be thinking always, what would Grantland Rice do? There's a real maker of myths. You know St. Paul's letter to the Corinthians? "You got all the runners in the stadium —"

MICHAEL

"Though all the runners enter the stadium, only one will win."

LOMBARDI

That's right. You know. Run to win.

(Turns to Michael, points his finger.)

Life is not without risks, Michael. Most writers are writing this one new fancy way, but it's only like a shiny toy and pretty soon it's going to break and fall apart. Don't follow them, Michael. Stick to the basics!

MICHAEL

Okay.

LOMBARDI

You may be the next maker of myths.

(A gust of wind. Lombardi looks up and around.)

Smell that? Something like a mix of fresh cut grass and burning leaves? I love that smell.

(Calling off:)

Phil, that's long enough for a scrimmage! Let's get to the wind sprints.

(To Michael:)

All I need is another injury.

(Looking off.)

Blow the whistle!

(Taylor enters.)

Where the hell are you going?

TAYLOR

Gonna take off my pads.

LOMBARDI

Well drop them here and get back on the damn field.

(As he exits:)

Phil! Blow the whistle! Jesus Katy. Do I have to do everything around here?

(He's off.)

MICHAEL

Hey, Jim.

TAYLOR

Roy.

MICHAEL

Five minutes. 'Sall I ask.

TAYLOR

I don't even got one minute.

MICHAEL

One minute then. All you have to do is answer yes or no. Are you thinking about leaving the Packers?

TAYLOR

I ain't talking to you.

MICHAEL

Why not? Why can't you talk to me?

LOMBARDI

(Off:)

Taylor!

TAYLOR

Get the hell away.

LOMBARDI

(Off:)

McCormick!

MICHAEL

Dammit.

(Jim trots off. Lombardi enters in a rage.)

LOMBARDI

What the hell do you think you're doing?!

MICHAEL

I'm taking your advice.

LOMBARDI

This is the second time I'm catching you! I specifically told you not to talk to Jim Taylor.

MICHAEL

But I'm just doing what any good journalist would do —

LOMBARDI

No, nothing doing Mister!

MICHAEL

Can I just talk to the man?

LOMBARDI

Get off this practice field!

MICHAEL

What!?

LOMBARDI

Get out and don't ever think about coming back!

(Michael looks around, sees all eyes are on him.)

What the hell are you waiting for?!

MICHAEL

But —

LOMBARDI

I don't let my players get away with breaking the rules, why should I let someone like you?! Damnit, you disappoint me, Michael. You were welcome as a guest, but you have abused that privilege. *Now get out!*

(Michael digs in his heels.)

MICHAEL

I'm a writer, I'm not one of your players! You can't treat me like a child —

LOMBARDI

That's it! Out!

MICHAEL

Gladly!

LOMBARDI

Tom Ryder's gonna hear about this!

MICHAEL

And I'm going to check into a hotel.

LOMBARDI

You got that right, Mister.

MICHAEL

I'm writing this story.

LOMBARDI

Get off the field!

MICHAEL

And you can't stop me!

LOMBARDI

Now!

(Michael walks away. Lombardi looks around.)

All right, folks, nothing to see here. Come on, boys, get back to work!

(He exits.)

MICHAEL

I don't know what it was. Something about the way Lombardi barked at me, and suddenly I was back in Jersey. A teenager, having it out with my father, never winning an argument. And in the corner of my eye I could see Dad, grinning. He would've taken Coach's side.

SCENE 10

(Lights shift to Robinson, a Green Bay Tavern. "Stand By Me" sung by the Drifters plays from a jukebox.)

ROBINSON

I knew Coach was a guard at Fordham, one of the Seven Blocks of Granite. Those guys were legendary, so I thought I was gonna be meeting a big man. Instead, I shake hands with this little squatty dude.

(Lights reveal a pool table. Michael and Robinson play as they talk. On a chair rests a couple of coats and a magazine.)

Then we start training camp, and I think, Why is this guy all over me? He is ranting and raving and he just won't let up. Then, like halfway through the season, I get it. It's when he leaves you *alone* — that's when you should start worrying. Means he's cutting you loose.

MICHAEL

Huh.

ROBINSON

Most of the guys he *wasn't* yelling at were gone by the first game of the season. See?

MICHAEL

So.

ROBINSON

You should feel honored, is all I'm saying. I never seen him lay into a civilian the way he laid into you today.

HORNUNG

(Entering, holding a beer.)

Hey, fellas!

ROBINSON

Horn! Look what the cat dragged in.

HORNUNG

I thought you might be on the next bus out.

ROBINSON

I'm trying to cheer him up.

HORNUNG

Man, Coach was all over you like white on rice.

ROBINSON

I told him it means the coach likes him.

HORNUNG

Yeah. Or he doesn't. One of those two.

MICHAEL

What *is* this place?

ROBINSON

Lombardi approved — you know, it's on the list. One of the first things Coach did when he came to Green Bay was let folks know that wherever any one of his players is not welcome, *all* his players are not welcome. This place's open for business to both Negroes and whites. Same applies to down south. When we're on the road, Coach makes sure we all stay in the same hotel.

HORNUNG

It's because he's been called a Wop all his life.

ROBINSON

Maybe.

HORNUNG

'S part of it.

ROBINSON

All I know is we all get treated the same around here.

HORNUNG/ROBINSON

Like dogs!

(They laugh.)

HORNUNG

Is that Jim over there?

ROBINSON

Yeah. I think he might be looking for me.

HORNUNG

That right?

ROBINSON

(To Michael:)

Almost every day, since the team elected me representative.

MICHAEL

Of what?

ROBINSON

Players' Association. We're meeting with the owners after the season. First time that's happened, ever, and Jim's got a bone to pick.

HORNUNG

Major bone.

(Taylor comes up to the table.)

Hey, Partner.

TAYLOR

Hey, Horn.

ROBINSON

Jim.

TAYLOR

Roy.

ROBINSON

You change your mind about granting this poor fella an interview?

TAYLOR

(Chuckles.)

Coach had a field day with you this afternoon. Jesus jumpin' cripes.

(Taylor takes a crumpled sheet of paper from his pocket.)

ROBINSON

Who'd you come with, Jim?

TAYLOR

No one.

ROBINSON

Never / seen you —

TAYLOR

I was — /

ROBINSON

What?

TAYLOR

Nothing. You told me to find you after practice.

ROBINSON

And here I am.

TAYLOR

Yeah, I got this — well, here.

(Hands him the list.)

ROBINSON

Are these grievances any different from the ones we talked about last week or the week before?

TAYLOR

Yeah. I added exhibition games. They got to pay us for those —

HORNUNG

That'd be good.

TAYLOR

No more working for free.

HORNUNG

I like that one, Robbie.

ROBINSON

Sure.

TAYLOR

The other stuff, medical insurance —

ROBINSON

Listen, Jim.

TAYLOR

— but I went into more detail down here. See, I got this friend who knows something about —

ROBINSON

Jim!

TAYLOR

What?

(Beat.)

ROBINSON

We will address all this stuff after the end of this season. This is a process. We ain't goddam cavemen anymore.

HORNUNG

Anyway, we ought to stay focused on this Sunday, right?

ROBINSON

Right.

TAYLOR

(To Robinson:)

No reason to raise your voice, Roy.

ROBINSON

I didn't raise my voice.

TAYLOR

Yes, you did.

HORNUNG

(Warning.)

Boys.

ROBINSON

(After a beat, re the list:)

Jim, I promise you I will absolutely address your concerns at the end of the season. I've got a list now. Okay?

TAYLOR

Alright.

HORNUNG

Hey Jim, why don't you stay a spell and play?

TAYLOR

Why not? 'Long as I'm here.

HORNUNG

You and Robbie versus me and Shakespeare.

TAYLOR

(Taylor picks up Robbie's magazine.)

Who's *Esquire*?

HORNUNG

Mine. You guys read this?

ROBINSON

Yup.

TAYLOR

I've been trying to buy a copy. Whole town's sold out.

ROBINSON

Mike, you know this guy who wrote that?

MICHAEL

No!

HORNUNG

What a hornswaggler.

MICHAEL

I had nothing to do with that article.

HORNUNG

After I read it, I got to wondering — why the hell'd Coach ever let you on the practice field to begin with?

ROBINSON

Damage control.

HORNUNG

How's that?

ROBINSON

He's Tom Ryder's boy.

HORNUNG

Ah-ha.

MICHAEL

What's that supposed to mean?

ROBINSON

Tom Ryder's like, practically Coach's own press agent. It's a cinch he sent you here to counteract this piece of crap.

MICHAEL

No.

ROBINSON

You didn't know that?

MICHAEL

It's not true. Mr. Ryder would never do that.

ROBINSON

I wouldn't be so sure.

HORNUNG

This just cuts him to shreds.

TAYLOR

It's pretty bad.

HORNUNG

You reporters just push a story about any which direction you like.

ROBINSON

What a jerk.

MICHAEL

That guy's just looking for attention.

HORNUNG

What about you, Mike?

MICHAEL

Hey, I like Coach Lombardi. I just wanted to get at *him*.

ROBINSON

He's not gonna let you do that.

HORNUNG

I been made to look like a genius in one paper and a complete idiot in another, all in the same day.

TAYLOR

I hate reporters.

ROBINSON

Of course, until you got a use for them.

TAYLOR

What's that supposed to mean?

ROBINSON

Nothing, Jim. Just —

TAYLOR

Hell, I got no need for this.

(He makes to leave.)

ROBINSON

Kidding, partner.

TAYLOR

That was a year ago. You keep bringing it up.

HORNUNG

Jim, wait. It's not a criticism, he was just making a point. More power to you, right Robbie?

ROBINSON

Absolutely.

TAYLOR

Okay.

(They all go back to the game.)

MICHAEL

What was that all about?

ROBINSON

You can tell him, Jim. He's not writing the story anymore, are you?

MICHAEL

... No.

TAYLOR

Huh.

ROBINSON

Go on, tell him.

MICHAEL

Off the record.

HORNUNG

Jim here decided one time to take negotiations outside the front office.

TAYLOR

My agent put me up to it. He said I would get results.

LOMBARDI

(From off:)

What the hell is this!

TAYLOR

All I did was tell the truth.

LOMBARDI

(Off:)

Taylor!

TAYLOR

On the last game of last year, which we lost. I was benched and I didn't know why.

LOMBARDI

(Enters, furious, holding a newspaper.)

Have you seen this, Taylor?

TAYLOR

It made me mad.

SCENE 11

(Lights full on Coach's office. Taylor steps into the scene.)

LOMBARDI

(Reads:)

"... and Jim Taylor suffered a frustrating day on the bench — "

TAYLOR

I was misquoted.

LOMBARDI

"— I asked him if the rumors were true that he was going to play out his contract and leave the Packers. 'Yes', was the terse reply from the big fullback, and he was gone." What part of "yes" was misquoted?

TAYLOR

I was embarrassed. I'm not used to the bench.

LOMBARDI

I don't care!

TAYLOR

I was playing my damndest, Coach!

LOMBARDI

You were slacking off.

TAYLOR

I was in pain.

LOMBARDI

So was Fuzz, so was Hawg. We all play through pain. Hell, I spent four years at Fordham in constant pain. You! I seen you play half a football game with your tongue half bitten through. Championship game against the Giants, nineteen-sixty-one. You spit out so much blood you turned pale. What changed?

TAYLOR

Doc said I was risking my career.

LOMBARDI

What doctor?

TAYLOR

Ours —

LOMBARDI

Never mind! It's beside the point. You got an issue with wanting to leave the Green Bay Packers, you take it directly to me and leave the press out of it. They'll eat you alive.

TAYLOR

I can handle myself.

LOMBARDI

(Waving his hand.)

No, you can't! You think they care about Jim Taylor or Vince Lombardi? I know these fellows and how they play the game and it's players like you they count on to mess up so they can get their promotion or bonus or whatever the hell it is they're after. Congratulations, Jim! You've been had.

(After a beat:)

How'd we become the Packers? How'd we turn this team around?

TAYLOR

Mental toughness.

LOMBARDI

No! Well, yeah, that's one way, but I was thinking of something else.

TAYLOR

Discipline.

LOMBARDI

Shut up! This is how. We're a team. No man bigger than any of the others. If I bench you it's not because I don't like you, but because I have a very good reason. Now, sit down.

(Taylor sits. Lombardi goes to him, puts his hand on his shoulder, rubs it a bit. His tone becomes more friendly.)

What's this about you wanting to leave the Packers?

TAYLOR

Don't want to leave, Coach. I want to be a Packer for as long as I play the game of football. This is my home and you know that, and I love the game and I love the boys and all the rest. I love getting up on Sundays and coming out into the cold and then going down to Lambeau and playing on that frozen field, even when it's ten below and the ball's so hard it feels like a brick against your gut. I love seeing Fuzzy and Jerry out in front of me, cross stepping round the end on the power sweep — hell, I love all that.

LOMBARDI

When I met you six years ago, you'd just about had it with football. I shook your hand and it felt like a limp fish. You shied away from reporters and barely spoke to anyone.

TAYLOR

I know.

LOMBARDI

Now I shake your hand and you just about pull me down to my knees.

TAYLOR

You give me confidence, Coach.

LOMBARDI

We did that together, Jim. So you have confidence. What's the problem?

TAYLOR

No problem. Well, maybe that was a mistake on your part to give me such a confidence. You sold me short last year.

LOMBARDI

We discuss contract in the spring, Mister!

TAYLOR

I do not wish to discuss it now. I do not wish to discuss it ever again.

LOMBARDI

Neither do I!

TAYLOR

I am only telling you that come next season, I will bring someone else to talk contract, not me.

LOMBARDI

What?! A damn lawyer?

TAYLOR

An agent maybe.

LOMBARDI

Pride! That's what we play for! That's what we used to play for when the game was a game and not a bunch of show business and reporters and all the rest of that malarkey! I created a monster.

TAYLOR

Goddamn it, Coach! Can't you see your way to moving one inch in anyone else's direction?!

LOMBARDI

That's it! Out!

TAYLOR

I'm not doing this from hunger. I'm only doing it to be fair.

LOMBARDI

What's that supposed to mean?

TAYLOR

We see these young kids come up from college getting ten times what we're getting paid.

LOMBARDI

I don't put a high stake in the cash part of the business and if you were smart, you'd do the same.

TAYLOR

You're telling me to act like a professional on the field, but not in my business affairs. I don't know how much you get paid and I don't really care. That's your business. But we're the ones out there taking the knocks, we're the ones with the four year careers and the chance to get hurt every time we step out on the field. We see the money coming in, but none of it winds up in our pockets. What we get paid doesn't matter once we're playing. We fight to win like we always do — you made us that way, Coach. But — hell, I don't know, I'm just talking about being fair.

(Pause.)

LOMBARDI

Jim, I do not wish to talk to your lawyer.

TAYLOR

Agent —

LOMBARDI

— whatever goddamn-gutter-crawling-creature you feel needs to be put in front of me! But if that's what it takes to keep you focused on the game, this is what I will do: You stay away from the press.

TAYLOR

Okay.

LOMBARDI

Forever.

TAYLOR

Huh?

LOMBARDI

Till the end of time.

(Beat.)

And I will talk to your agent.

(Taylor thinks.)

And if you do *not* accept this offer, I will trade you immediately. As soon as your ass hits that door, you will be on a bus to Philly or Cleveland or L.A. or wherever, I don't care. You understand?

TAYLOR

Okay.

LOMBARDI

Okay what?

TAYLOR

I will stay a Packer.

LOMBARDI

We don't exactly see eye to eye, Jim, but we push each other, don't we?

TAYLOR

I guess so.

LOMBARDI

We push each other to the brink and that's not for nothing, is it?

TAYLOR

I guess not.

LOMBARDI

Good. Get out!

SCENE 12

(Lights restore back to the Tavern and the pool game. Jim rejoins the men.)

TAYLOR

I got sick of being played for a sucker, that's all.

ROBINSON

Players' Association's got a plan now. No one's going to be taken advantage of.

HORNUNG

Only time I feel like a sucker is when we lose.

ROBINSON

Got to have both, Horn. Pride both on the field and off.

HORNUNG

All I know is, I don't want to play for any man other than Coach Lombardi.

TAYLOR

I could do without all the piss and vinegar.

HORNUNG

I wouldn't trade one season with Lombardi for ten seasons and a million dollars anywhere else.

TAYLOR

A million dollars is a lot of money.

ROBINSON

But you'd never be as good on any other team.

HORNUNG

True.

TAYLOR

Maybe.

ROBINSON

You know what I want to do?

MICHAEL

What?

ROBINSON

I wanna — I want to get to just one game of perfection. One game where he can't say a single thing that I did wrong.

TAYLOR

Good luck.

MICHAEL

I envy you guys.

HORNUNG

Why? You got talents.

MICHAEL

I was never good at sports.

HORNUNG

I can't write. You got something I don't have.

MICHAEL

Maybe.

HORNUNG

You write the stories folks will read a hundred years from now. I play, you write.

ROBINSON

Anybody know how Starr is doing?

HORNUNG

I don't know.

TAYLOR

Got me.

MICHAEL

Starr plays hurt. He won't sit out. I got the statistics on that.

ROBINSON

You got the stats, do you?

MICHAEL

He's missed one start in the last thirty-three games.

ROBINSON

Well, what are the stats on Jim Taylor?

MICHAEL

Which year?

TAYLOR

Nineteen-sixty-two.

MICHAEL

League MVP: one thousand-four-hundred-seventy-four yards, five-point-four yards per carry, nineteen touchdowns. Dave "Robbie" Robinson: rookie season, switched from defensive end to outside linebacker. Second game of second season, returned his first interception eighty-six yards for a touchdown.

HORNUNG

This guy's good.

MICHAEL

Paul Hornung: one-hundred-seventy-six total points in nineteen-sixty, league MVP nineteen-sixty-one. Missed some of the sixty-two season due to the Cuban missile crisis.

HORNUNG

Jesus.

MICHAEL

On leave from army reserves you said to your teammates in a pre-game speech.

ROBINSON

Oh brother.

MICHAEL

(His best Paul Hornung:)

Fellas, I'm really happy to be here and I really needed this weekend more than a lot of you. I came here for two things. I took care of the first one last night —

ALL

— Now let's take care of the second and kick the shit out of the Forty-niners!

MICHAEL

I know more about all of you than you know about yourselves.

ROBINSON

You think so, huh?

MICHAEL

I know so.

TAYLOR

What else don't we know about Bart Starr?

MICHAEL

He'll play!

HORNUNG

He'll play and we'll win.

MICHAEL

We'll win!

ROBINSON

He won't play, and we'll still win!

HORNUNG

We'll win, goddammit!

TAYLOR

We'll win goddammit!

MICHAEL

You're the Packehs!

(A big cheer. Music up loud. Lights fade.)

SCENE 13

(A projector whirls. Vince Lombardi, in bathrobe, stands next to the projector.)

LOMBARDI

(To himself:)

No no no no Skoronski, use your head!

MICHAEL

(Off:)

Oops.

LOMBARDI

Hey!

(He turns off the projector.)

MICHAEL

(Entering:)

Sorry.

LOMBARDI

Watch it, Mister.

MICHAEL

Sorry!

LOMBARDI

Keep your voice down, Marie's sleeping.

MICHAEL

(Whispers.)

I just came back for my things.

LOMBARDI

Don't be a fool, McCormick. It's nearly three in the morning. Have you been drinking?

MICHAEL

I might have had a few.

LOMBARDI

Were you out with Paul?! Don't answer that, I don't want to know.

MICHAEL

Okay.

LOMBARDI

Michael, I — um. I want to say that I, I shouldn't have yelled at you today.

MICHAEL

I think I might have had it coming.

LOMBARDI

That's true, but I may have gone a little too far. I have a temper. Well, you know it, and Marie tells me all the time, and my children. It's a problem and I can't seem to fix it.

(Michael waits for more.)

I go to mass at St. Willebrord's every morning and I pray for patience, for understanding. But it never helps.

(Beat, then…)

MICHAEL

I'm sorry I woke you.

LOMBARDI

I was up. Listen, I spoke to Tom tonight, Tom Ryder. I want to make sure you and I have had a chance to review your article. When are you scheduled to leave?

MICHAEL

You — I'm sorry, what?

LOMBARDI

I don't want you to leave without me seeing what you wrote.

MICHAEL

The guys were right.

LOMBARDI

What guys?

MICHAEL

Coach, I can't do that.

LOMBARDI

Yes, you can.

MICHAEL

No, you don't understand, Coach, I *don't* do that. It's not what a reporter does.

LOMBARDI

That was the deal from the start.

MICHAEL

No, it wasn't.

LOMBARDI

Tom Ryder and I have an agreement with your magazine that nothing gets printed without my say so.

MICHAEL

No!

LOMBARDI

Sh!

MICHAEL

(Whisper-shouts.)

Sorry.

LOMBARDI

Keep your voice down!

MICHAEL

Sorry! This is crazy! That was never discussed. That was not a part of this —

(Michael takes it all in.)

I can't believe this. Who does that? / What self-respecting newspaperman —

LOMBARDI

Now settle down, Mike. / Maybe you didn't realize it, but that's the only way I would agree to this sort of thing.

MICHAEL

Well, I won't write it then.

LOMBARDI

(Yelling:)

What do you mean you won't write it!

MICHAEL

Sh!

LOMBARDI

(Barely softer:)

Why the hell have I been catering to you this whole week long?!

MICHAEL

You kicked me off your practice field today!

LOMBARDI

I apologized for that.

MICHAEL

Actually —

LOMBARDI

And you deserved it!

MICHAEL

— Actually, you didn't apologize. You said something that / sounded like an —

LOMBARDI

Hey hey hey! / All right, that's enough!

MICHAEL/LOMBARDI

Ssssshhhhhh!

(Beat.)

LOMBARDI

Quit then, dammit. Tom Ryder isn't going to be too happy.

MICHAEL

He can write it himself.

LOMBARDI

Are you prepared to lose your job?

MICHAEL

… I don't know.

LOMBARDI

I'd think about all this if I were you.

(Michael sits, stares at the projector.)

I didn't mean now.

MICHAEL

(Re: the projector.)

Am I keeping you from this?

LOMBARDI

I think I'm done.

MICHAEL

You review films every single night?

LOMBARDI

No. Sometimes I — um, read cookbooks.

MICHAEL

You cook?

LOMBARDI

Not on your life, Mister, but it relaxes me. Sometimes I find a nice glazed ham and it helps me forget. I got to do something. Every night, I'm wide awake at three a.m.

(Lombardi removes a bottle of Pepto-Bismol from his robe and sips from it the rest of the scene.)

MICHAEL

I haven't been sleeping well.

LOMBARDI

I have the game. What's your excuse?

MICHAEL

Writers don't have stress?

LOMBARDI

I wouldn't know. Even when I had a straight job, all those years teaching chemistry and physics, I was coaching football in the evenings. Football works on your nerves.

MICHAEL

When I was at Ignatius, the Fathers had us on very strict schedules.

LOMBARDI

That's the Jesuit way.

MICHAEL

I hated it.

LOMBARDI

I loved it.

MICHAEL

Though you know, it probably made me a better writer.

LOMBARDI

I liked the challenge. My Mother had to have everything just right. She drove me that way, and if I didn't meet expectations, she'd smack me one and make me start all over again.

MICHAEL

My dad was pretty tough on me.

LOMBARDI

Your dad struck me as the kind of a fellow who wouldn't let much slip past him.

MICHAEL

You got that right.

LOMBARDI

He was a good man, a fair man, and he treated you with respect.

MICHAEL

He wanted me to be a lawyer.

LOMBARDI

Huh.

MICHAEL

But I wanted to be a newspaperman, just like him. You'd think he would be proud, but no... Boy, he never let up, always told me how much I was messing up.

LOMBARDI

He had expectations.

MICHAEL

Brutal.

LOMBARDI

Like my ma.

MICHAEL

What about your son?

LOMBARDI

Vincent?

MICHAEL

Yeah.

LOMBARDI

That boy is stubborn, I'll tell you. He never listened. He wanted to be a football coach, but I told him if he chose that profession, he'd never get a dime from me.

MICHAEL

Sounds familiar.

LOMBARDI

You want the best for your son, but I — I guess I never had an aptitude for getting through to Vincent. I just don't understand the boy.

MICHAEL

What would you rather see him be?

LOMBARDI

Lawyer.

(He smiles.)

This game coming up is killing me. That middle linebacker, fifty-one, is giving me nightmares.

MICHAEL

The way I see it, you don't win this week, you still got next week.

LOMBARDI

I don't think that way. This game is what I got in front of me. This is what I've got to do this week, this day, this minute.

MICHAEL

"Winning isn't everything. It's the only thing."

LOMBARDI

Something like that.

MICHAEL

You know, everyone thinks you thought that up.

LOMBARDI

I never said I did.

MICHAEL

But I tracked it all the way back to a movie starring John Wayne.

LOMBARDI

Huh.

MICHAEL

And guess who says it? His eleven year-old daughter.

LOMBARDI

I'll be damned.

MICHAEL

To a social worker played by Donna Reed.

LOMBARDI

Point is, most people misinterpret it. It's supposed to be about focus. If you want something badly enough, you've got to be single-minded about it. A man doesn't do anything to win — cheat, whatever. Winning is an attitude. I know losing is a part of life. Doesn't mean I have to like it…

(Re the projector:)

Take these game films. Sometimes all I can do is see the mistakes. And when I go to bed, I lie there going over the games and the plays, the real games and plays that will never change no matter how many times I go over them. Nights like tonight, Vincent? I am in hell.

(Beat, then…)

MICHAEL

Michael.

LOMBARDI

Huh?

MICHAEL

I'm…

(Another beat.)

Professor of Abnormal Psychology is just finishing a lecture on mental health and he follows that with an oral quiz for his class. He asks them, "How would you diagnose a patient who walks back and forth screaming at the top of his lungs one minute, and then sits in a chair sobbing uncontrollably?" No one answers for awhile till finally a student in the back of the room whips up his hand and says "Football Coach!"

(Lombardi throws back his head and laughs.)

LOMBARDI

Good one.

MICHAEL

You can't control the way your players play.

LOMBARDI

Yes, I can.

MICHAEL

They're going to make mistakes.

LOMBARDI

And they do.

MICHAEL

And they're going to have minds of their own.

LOMBARDI

Not if I have anything to say about it. But you're right. I am unfortunate in that what I do for a living depends on other men.

(Beat.)

You should feel lucky.

MICHAEL

I don't.

LOMBARDI

Your success depends on you alone.

MICHAEL

Except of course when your editor is working with your subject to change it to his satisfaction.

(Lombardi laughs.)

LOMBARDI

Touche'.

MICHAEL

Well?

LOMBARDI

Tom Ryder is a friend of mine.

MICHAEL

I'm not saying he isn't.

LOMBARDI

You work for the man. You should respect him.

MICHAEL

What makes you think I don't?

LOMBARDI

Then let him do his job. And you do your job, which is to follow his lead. See, this is what I'm talking about. Young people today, they just don't respect their leaders.

MICHAEL

I don't think —

LOMBARDI

You listen to me. There's something going on these days and I don't know how it got started. My son is like this. He never listened to me and I think it has to do with the way this country is going. People don't respect authority anymore.

MICHAEL

Not everyone is comfortable following orders.

LOMBARDI

In that case… it is that individual's responsibility to get himself out of that position. Maybe that individual is a leader and not a follower. It's hard to find a good leader. In fact, most people in this world are followers.

MICHAEL

Not in America.

LOMBARDI

Especially in America. Maybe you are not among them.

MICHAEL

I just don't like people messing with my work. And I hate editors.

LOMBARDI

Well.

MICHAEL

Yes?

LOMBARDI

Then you've got a problem.

(Marie enters; Lombardi sees her.)

Aw, jeez.

MARIE

Is anyone ever going to go to bed?

LOMBARDI

I can't sleep.

MARIE

Big surprise. Michael, were you out with Paul?

MICHAEL

How'd you guess?

MARIE

That boy's got a reputation to uphold.

LOMBARDI

I better not catch him standing at a bar, that's all I can say.

MARIE

And if you do, what then?

LOMBARDI

Don't worry, it'll never happen.

MARIE

Because you'll make sure you never catch him.

(To Mike:)

Vince wants to *be* Paul. That's the big secret.

LOMBARDI

Shut up, Marie.

MICHAEL

Maybe he's the other side of Vince Lombardi.

LOMBARDI

(Thinks.)

Maybe.

MARIE

Are you coming to bed?

VINCE

In a minute.

MARIE

I'm sorry my husband embarrassed you at practice today, Michael.

MICHAEL

Does everybody know?

MARIE

Only all of Green Bay, but don't worry, it's a very small municipality. Good night.

(She exits.)

LOMBARDI

Michael, what are you going to do about your article?

MICHAEL

I don't know. Write it, I guess.

LOMBARDI

It's part of my job — everything that has to do with the Green Bay Packers lands on my desk. I have a responsibility.

MICHAEL

So do I.

LOMBARDI

What's that?

MICHAEL

To my writing. To myself.

LOMBARDI

Well.

(Beat.)

May the best man win.

(Lights dim as we hear stadium cheers.)

SCENE 14

(Game day. Crowd sounds, a band. The Packer Locker room. Paul and Jim, dressed in full Packer regalia.)

HORNUNG

Hey, Jim.

TAYLOR

What's up, Horn?

HORNUNG

Did Robbie tell you?

TAYLOR

Tell me what?

HORNUNG

Where the hell'd he go now?

TAYLOR

He was barfing in the toilet when I saw him a couple minutes ago.

HORNUNG

Some things never change.

TAYLOR

What did he need to tell me?

HORNUNG

Number fifty-one. He's hurting.

ROBINSON

(Enters, also dressed to play.)

I saw him warming up. He's limping on that left leg and trying to hide it.

TAYLOR

Does Bart know?

ROBINSON

I told him.

HORNUNG

So we'll run the sweep off the weak side first part of the game. Take it right to him.

TAYLOR

Left side right side. Healthy, hurt, don't matter to me. How's your stomach, Robbie?

ROBINSON

Better.

TAYLOR

You want a shot at that ring?

ROBINSON

Hell, yeah!

TAYLOR

Then let's get to it!

(Lights shift to under the Lambeau stands. Michael and Marie enter.)

MICHAEL

Almost kick-off.

MARIE

You know, I haven't missed one of Vince's games in twenty years — wait, I take that back. I missed one in San Francisco. His brother Harold lives there and we went shopping instead.

MICHAEL

I didn't know he had a brother in San Francisco.

MARIE

Nothing like my husband, though Vince adores him. But Harold won't go near a football field.

MICHAEL

So you spent the afternoon with him?

MARIE

Yes. And the Packers lost. I'd made Vince unlucky by my absence. So I come, every Sunday, rain or shine. Doesn't stop Vince from forgetting I was there and leaving without me after the game. That's happened more than once.

(She turns to Michael.)

It was nice to have you here this week Michael, a little breath of Manhattan. You broke up a very monotonous yet distressing routine. I'm glad you decided to stay.

MICHAEL

Me too.

MARIE

No offense, but I didn't think you'd last.

(Starter pistol, cheers. Marie exits, lights shift, Michael speaks to us. We see images of the game.)

MICHAEL

I watched the game from the sidelines. It was a defensive battle at first, the Packers pushing back a lean and powerful arch rival.

(Lombardi appears in a light, wearing his trademark camel hair coat, hat and galoshes. He paces.)

LOMBARDI

What kind of football are we playing out there today!

MICHAEL

The ball changed hands five times before anyone had a chance to score.

LOMBARDI

What the hell is going on out here?!

MICHAEL

It was then that the Packers got inside the twenty yard-line. Bart Starr handed off to Paul Hornung and the sweep was on. With Jerry Kramer leading the way, Hornung darted around four tacklers before he was finally brought down on the three yard-line. And then he did not get up, and the crowd went quiet. After a while, he was helped off the field, and he spent the rest of the game on the bench.

LOMBARDI

Come on, boys, back to work!

MICHAEL

A Packer field goal attempt was blocked. The rest of the first half, Bart Starr and company came close to scoring, but were thwarted by that big linebacker Lombardi had been carping about all week long. And the defense wasn't doing much better.

LOMBARDI

You call that a tackle?! You barely touched him!

MICHAEL

Though they never tired, the Packers made mistakes. They were human.

LOMBARDI

It's not called grabbing, it's called tackling! Grab grab grab! Play the goddam game!

MICHAEL

All game long, I saw Lombardi send in only two or three plays. But mostly he just paced the sidelines, hands behind his back, fidgetting. His team was so well prepared that once the game had started, he was the most useless man on the field.

LOMBARDI

Look to it, now, boys. Come on, Bart!

MICHAEL

Then things turned around in the second half. Bart Starr was virtually flawless, completing eleven of twelve passes. Jim Taylor ran for ninety-two yards and scored the go-ahead touchdown.

(Roar of a crowd. Footage of Taylor scoring on the Sweep.)

In the final seconds, with the Packers leading by three, the opposing team was driving down the field when Big Dave Robinson came out of nowhere to make the game-saving sack.

(Starter pistol. Cheers.)

BROADCASTER VOICE #1

The Packers win! The Packers win! And they will take the Western Division Conference, Ladies and Gentlemen, earning their first trip to the National Championship in three years…

(Lights shift to the Locker Room. Dave Robinson, in a tattered Green Bay uniform, meets up with a limping, and dressed, Paul Hornung.)

HORNUNG

Good one, Robbie. That last tackle? You saved our asses.

ROBINSON

Thanks, Horn.

(They spot Lombardi, who enters. Paul goes to him.)

HORNUNG

Congratulations, Coach.

LOMBARDI

Next week, Paul. You'll be back.

HORNUNG

Don't I know it.

(He exits.)

LOMBARDI

Good game, Jim. How to go.

TAYLOR

Thanks, Coach.

(Taylor exits the opposite direction. Lombardi approaches Robinson, who waits. Lombardi hugs him.)

LOMBARDI

Robbie, that last sack.

ROBINSON

(Smiling.)

Yes, Coach?

LOMBARDI

(Frowns.)

You should not have been blitzing.

(He exits. Lights shift to a tunnel underneath the stadium. Paul runs into Michael.)

HORNUNG

Hey, champ.

MICHAEL

How's the knee?

HORNUNG

Bag of tricks. Wish you could've caught a different game. You sure you can't stick around for another week?

MICHAEL

Sorry, Paul.

HORNUNG

Next time, then. You want to come out for a drink? Me and McGee got a couple airline stewardesses waiting on us. I'm sure they could scare up a stray sister or ugly cousin or something.

MICHAEL

I got to write this story.

HORNUNG

Suit yourself, Pal. Now don't you forget to treat me kindly.

MICHAEL

Sure thing, Paul.

HORNUNG

Hey, Mr. Reporter — You got my reputation to uphold.

(He smiles. As he limps off, he passes Marie.)

MARIE

Paul! Paul, is my husband still here?

HORNUNG

He was wearing his coat and hat when he left.

MARIE

Tough break today.

HORNUNG

Yes, ma'am.

MARIE

You're still my boy.

(Paul exits. Marie continues on her way. As she leaves:)

Michael, are you coming to the party? I've got a cream cheese crab dip that's to die for.

(And she's off.)

MICHAEL

(To us:)

I went back to the Lombardi's, but not for the rec room party. I stayed upstairs, out of sight, quietly packed my bags, and then made myself scarce. Checked into a YMCA and started writing. A few hours later, I'd finished my story and had everything but the title. I tried to think of something appropriate, some recurring theme of the week. *Shut up Marie* came to mind. Then I thought, let Ryder give it a title. Let him figure it out.

SCENE 15

(Post-party, the Lombardi home. Lombardi stands before Marie, his audience. Both hold Manhattans.)

LOMBARDI

Okay, so there's this teacher and he's talking to his class. And they're all listening, he's —

(Michael walks in.)

Wait. Who's a teacher, a psychiatrist or a psychologist?

MARIE

Either could be.

MICHAEL

Psychologist.

LOMBARDI

Michael! Just in time, I'm telling Marie your joke. This teacher's teaching the class — no, he finishes the class, but he wants to test the kids so he does a pop quiz — well, not exactly a pop quiz. It's, well, it's a review — doesn't matter! So he says who is the guy, the certain guy, who screams and hollers and then sits down right away, and a kid from way in the back says 'A football coach'!

(Lombardi throws back his head and laughs. Marie just look at him.)

MARIE

I don't get it.

LOMBARDI

You're crazy. It's the funniest joke I've heard in weeks.

MARIE

It's lost on me.

LOMBARDI

Michael —

MARIE

That's all I can say.

LOMBARDI

Michael, come on in and have a drink.

MICHAEL

Everyone's left already?

LOMBARDI

It's nearly ten o'clock. What did you expect?

MARIE

Where have you been?

LOMBARDI

You missed a good one.

MICHAEL

(Re: his papers.)

I had to get this done, so I needed to find a place I could write.

LOMBARDI

What is it?

MICHAEL

My article.

MARIE

Already?

MICHAEL

Finished. I wanted you to read it.

(He hands Lombardi the pages.)

LOMBARDI

The two of us will go over this tonight.

MICHAEL

No, thanks. The way this is right now is my last draft. I'm just guessing you won't like it, and maybe I won't like your changes, so let's just say I wrote this, I did my job, and you will do your job. And I quit.

MARIE

Quit what?

MICHAEL

Look Magazine.

MARIE

No!

MICHAEL

I just phoned Mr. Ryder. Left a message with his service.

MARIE

But you just started working for them.

MICHAEL

I know. I appreciate the chance, and I didn't want to be dramatic —

MARIE

Well, you are.

MICHAEL

But I think —

MARIE

You're being *very* dramatic.

MICHAEL

Sorry...

MARIE

No, go on Michael. This is interesting.

MICHAEL

I just don't think this is what I should be doing.

LOMBARDI

You know, Michael, if you were on my team, I'd be happy to see you go.

MICHAEL

I know you would.

LOMBARDI

Ha!

(Lombardi shakes his hand.)

Congratulations.

MICHAEL

Thank you.

LOMBARDI

Let's celebrate! Marie, Michael here's about to take matters into his own hands. Isn't that right?

MARIE

Wonderful.

MICHAEL

And if it doesn't work out —

LOMBARDI

It'll work out.

MARIE

It'll work out. But I hope you're not going to give up writing.

MICHAEL

No.

MARIE

Good. That would be a waste of talent.

LOMBARDI

I think you should be like your dad. Find a small time operation and have the run of the place.

MICHAEL

Sounds nice, but I think I might try something a little different.

MARIE

Like what?

MICHAEL

Books.

LOMBARDI

Well — let's drink to it.

MARIE

Let me get you a Manhattan.

(She goes to the bar.)

MICHAEL

No, thanks, I —

LOMBARDI

Have a drink, dammit!

MICHAEL

Okay!

LOMBARDI

(Laughs.)

That's the spirit! You gotta come down here sometime when you're not on the clock, maybe in the off-season, to see how things are when we're not in this type of a situation. When everything is on the line.

(Marie returns with a drink, hands it to Michael.)

Right, Marie?

MARIE

Right.

LOMBARDI

I'd invite you to stay on, but next week we're off to the west coast. Los Angeles has that young quarterback, Roman Gabriel.

MARIE

That's right.

(Lights start to iris in on Vince and Marie, who's settled close to her husband.)

LOMBARDI

And he's going to be our biggest challenge. Him, and that big defensive line. God almighty, I've got a lot of injured players, and I have got to think about what I'm going to do if... if...

(By now, Michael is out of our focus, and Vince's consciousness. The coach once again turns inward.)

MARIE

Vin.

LOMBARDI

Huh?

(But he's gone.)

MARIE

Nevermind.

(She doesn't move. Silence, then...)

LOMBARDI

I've got to get them up... but how?

(Vince sits there, lost in thought. Lights shift as Michael speaks to us.)

EPILOGUE

MICHAEL

Lombardi read my article and suggested no changes. And then Tom Ryder never printed it... he called later to say he didn't think it was what his readers might expect from *Look* Magazine. Too much art, not enough sports.

(Beat.)

Lombardi's Packers won the championship that year, and then the next, and then the next — three in a row. It'd never been done before. Five championships in seven years. Not bad. The first two Superbowl wins were Lombardi's and now that game's trophy is named after him. In nineteen-sixty-eight, Lombardi finally got burnt out on coaching and broke the hearts of Packer fans everywhere by quitting. Then he broke their hearts a second time by regretting his decision and accepting an offer to coach the Washington Redskins. And once again, he turned a losing franchise into a winning one, all in the space of a year.

(Beat.)

He probably would have turned that team into Superbowl champions if it weren't for the cancer, the colon cancer that had been devouring him slowly for years, and then quickly, at the age of fifty-seven. One opponent Vince Lombardi wasn't going to beat.

(Lights on Lombardi come up full. We see he's holding a football, as at the top of the show. Post-game, he addresses his Players.)

LOMBARDI

Gentleman, first I want to remind you all that this is not the end of the season.

MICHAEL

Many of his players came to his bedside to say their final farewells. And after he died, they never forgot him.

LOMBARDI

We have another two games left on the schedule…

MICHAEL

I never forgot him. Hell, who could?

LOMBARDI

… and I do not intend on slacking off just because we are guaranteed a shot at the championship.

MICHAEL

The most imperfect, perfect man I ever met.

(Lights fade on Michael.)

LOMBARDI

Now. I want to say that the team I saw out there today is exactly the team I expect to see all the time. Bart Starr, my God, out there playing with a torn ligament. We had a few other injuries, and we were not perfect. But you played selflessly and with a quiet determination that befits a championship team. I am especially proud — especially proud — of the way all you veterans pulled together this afternoon. All of you who were with this organization before the fifty-nine season, when things weren't exactly moving in the right direction. You never gave up on yourself, and, more importantly, you never gave up on one another. And that makes me proud. After all, the measure of a man is not in how he falls down, but how he pulls himself up off the ground. Anybody… Gentlemen, anybody can love something that is beautiful or bright or glamorous. But it takes a special person to love something imperfect and unknown. That is the true test of a person. You might have a guy playing next to you that isn't perfect, but you've got to love him, and maybe that will enable you to overcome a difficult situation because of that love.

(He looks down at the ball.)

About this time I give the game ball to an individual who has shown exemplary effort or courage during the game. Today, however, it goes to no one in particular, and to all of you in general. Two reasons. Because you deserve it, and second, we're not finished. I guess… I guess we'll never *be* finished, will we?

(Beat.)

Good night. That is all.

(Blackout.)

ERIC SIMONSON is a company member of Steppenwolf Theatre in Chicago. His plays include *Louder Faster* (with Jeffrey Hatcher), *Fake, Honest*, *Speak American*, *The Only Thing*, *Carter's Way*, *Work Song: Three Views of Frank Lloyd Wright* (also with Jeffrey Hatcher). Adaptations include *Slaughterhouse-Five*, and *Bang the Drum Slowly*. He writes for television and frequently directs plays, film, opera and documentaries. He is the recipient of a Tony nomination for directing *The Song of Jacob Zulu*; an Emmy nomination for his film *On Tiptoe: Gentle Steps to Freedom*; and the winner of an Academy Award for his documentary *A Note of Triumph: The Golden Age of Norman Corwin*. He lives in Los Angeles with his son, Henry.

A Production in Print is a production as a book.

For more information about Productions in Print go to www.inanhourbooks.com.

Your play can lead a double life — a life as a performance and a life as a book! Find out how today.